Let Me Go There

Also by the same author and available from Canterbury Press:

The Meaning is in the Waiting: The Spirit of Advent

This Risen Existence: The Spirit of Easter

Everyday God: The Spirit of the Ordinary

www.canterburypress.co.uk

Let Me Go There

The Spirit of Lent

Paula Gooder

CANTERBURY
PRESS
Norwich

First published in 2016 by the Canterbury Press Norwich
Editorial office
3rd Floor, Invicta House
108–114 Golden Lane
London EC1Y 0TG, UK

Second impression 2017

Hymns Ancient & Modern® is a registered trademark of Hymns Ancient and
Modern Ltd.

Canterbury Press is an imprint of Hymns Ancient & Modern
Ltd (a registered charity)
13A Hellesdon Park Road, Norwich,
Norfolk NR6 5DR, UK

www.canterburypress.co.uk

British Library Cataloguing in Publication data

A catalogue record for this book is available
from the British Library

978 1 84825 904 1

Printed and bound in Great Britain by
CPI Group (UK) Ltd, Croydon

For David Runcorn,
A sure guide through the wilderness

Contents

How to Read this Book

This is the last in a short series of books that I have written reflecting on key seasons in the Christian year. The first three explored Advent, Easter and Ordinary time, so it feels right to end the series with a book of reflections for Lent.

I chose as the theme for this book what I perceive to be two interlocking themes – Jesus' temptations in the wilderness and his calling of disciples. These two events stand next to each other at the very start of Jesus' ministry and begin to give us clues not only into who Jesus was and what he had come to do, but also into the importance of disciples to this ministry. The forty days of Lent, which mimic the forty days and nights Jesus spent in the wilderness, are a traditional focus for Lenten reflection not only because they reveal to us the deep nature of Jesus, but also because they give us a pattern to follow. The question is what kind of pattern do they offer? It is this question asked through a series of reflections on key Bible passages, that shapes the content of this book.

It begins with the theme of wilderness and why the wilderness was so important in the mind of the New Testament writers before, turning to the temptation narratives in each of the Gospels of Mark, Matthew and Luke. The book ends with two chapters on discipleship – the call and then the character and cost of discipleship. As with the other three books in this series, I have anchored the themes in 34 different biblical passages or verses as a means of exploring the text in more detail. It is important to bear in mind that the intention of this book is not to provide a list of easy and definitive answers but to be reflective, to stimulate your own thoughts and reflections on the subjects explored as a companion on the way through Lent.

You may be wondering why I have chosen the slightly odd number of 34 reflections. The answer is that it was a pragmatic choice. People count the forty days of Lent differently. Some include the whole sweep of days from Ash Wednesday until Holy Saturday but exclude Sundays; others include Sundays but end before the start of Holy Week. This book assumes that if you decide to read a reflection a day you can then leave out Sundays (or another day in the week) and stop as Holy Week begins, on the grounds that you will probably by then be wanting to turn your attention, reflections and devotions on to Jesus' death and resurrection. It also allows people like me, who have maybe slipped a day or two in their Lenten devotions, to catch up and still finish on time. You also need to be aware that to fit 34 reflections into six chapters meant that while most chapters have six reflections in them, two have five for reasons of simple mathematics.

I have written the reflections into chapters with introductions and conclusions for people who like to join the dots and see bigger pictures of what is going on, but if you prefer you can ignore these and just read the individual reflections (and join up your own dots!). You also don't need to read the book in order if you prefer to follow your own path through the passages.

One other note for people who have read other books in this series: in other books I began many of the reflections with some kind of anecdote before moving on to the passage. For reasons I don't understand, I just couldn't do that this time. I tried and tried and in the end gave up because they simply wouldn't come, or didn't sit well with the other material. One thing I have learnt in writing is that books take on a life of their own. You can shape and nudge them as you write but there are certain elements that simply will not change no matter how hard you try. So this comes by way of apology for those who prefer the anecdotes, I did try!

People who have read the other books in this series have asked me two things in particular – one was whether the daily readings could be numbered to make it easier to find out where you are, and the other was whether I could provide questions for small-group discussion in case anyone wanted to use the book in a Bible study context. I have done this and hope that people find them helpful. The questions assume that people have read each chapter and are designed to provide variety to stimulate discussion, but there is no need to answer them all nor, indeed, to stick with them if your conversation takes you into other interesting territory. I have given suggestions for reading the Bible together as well as discussion questions, but have left it to you how you begin and end, and how you pray, since groups often do this quite differently from one another.

I have also, as in the other books, written an opening reflection – this time on wilderness and discipleship – as a lens through which to see the issues in the rest of the book. You can read the book without it, but if you have the time and inclination you could read it before Lent begins by way of preparation. The opening reflection ends with an R. S. Thomas poem – 'The Coming' – which for me encapsulates what this book is really about.

However you use this book – whether you read it all or just some of it; whether you stop at the introduction or read only those reflections that appeal to you; whether you use it to journey through the whole of Lent or dip into it from time to time – I hope that this Lent you will discover again, as though for the first time, the joy of hearing that call – 'Come, follow me' – and of living out, in everything that you do, the patient following, learning and proclaiming that lie at the heart of discipleship.

INTRODUCTION
On Lent, the Wilderness and Discipleship

The ambiguity of the wilderness

I will never forget my first experience of wilderness. I was on a visit to the Holy Land and went out to the desert near the Dead Sea. I fell asleep in the bus on the outskirts of Jerusalem and woke, bleary-eyed, to find myself in what felt like a different world. It was the middle of summer and the sun's rays beat down on an already scorched landscape. The air above the sand shimmered in the heat. Sand stretched as far as the eye could see, broken only by the odd scrubby plant that rose dusty yet defiant from the arid earth.

That first experience of the desert had a powerful effect on me in a number of ways, but what struck me most about the territory was its ambiguity: it was at the same time alien and familiar; forbidding and inviting; lifeless and life-giving. We didn't stay for long. We were on a tight timetable. But the wilderness remained with me long after we left. Nearly 30 years later the emotional memory lingers on, especially when I read passages about it from the Bible.

It is not hard to see why the wilderness occupies the place it does in the popular imagination of the biblical writers. The desert was where people, like Hagar and Ishmael, were cast out and abandoned (see Genesis 16.1–16); it was also the place in which they met God and were saved (see Genesis 16.17–20). It was where God's people found refuge and protection from their Egyptian oppressors (see Exodus 16.1ff); it was also the place where they feared they would die from hunger (Exodus 16.3). The people of God entered the promised land through the wilderness and left through it again as they went into exile hundreds of years later. The wilderness was great and terrible (Deuteronomy 1.19). The wilderness was where God was expected to return (Isaiah 40.3).

Wilderness, both as a location and as a theme, runs all the way through the Old Testament and onwards into the New Testament. Its symbolic significance is one that we will explore in different ways, through the lens of different passages as this book unfolds. All the way through it remains a place of ambiguity, bringing both danger and salvation.

Lent is a season that invites us to step into the wilderness with all its ambiguity. It challenges us to be courageous and face the vulnerabilities we might naturally shy away from. It summons us to learn lessons about ourselves: who we are and who God calls us to be. It suggests that while what we fear most might sometimes bring exactly what we expect, at other times it can bring salvation and hope. There is no easy way through the wilderness; no shortcut route to take. Entering the wilderness takes courage and strength of heart, and we are not always able or strong enough to tackle it, but when we are able and strong enough we can find in it not bleakness but spaciousness; not terror but hope; not disaster but the very salvation we crave.

The wilderness and lent

It is a natural part of human nature to attempt to avoid places of danger and risk. This is especially true in today's risk-averse world which encourages us to be 'safe', to take no risks, to avoid danger whenever and however we can. The problem with this is that a 'safe' life is a small one. A life in which all risk is eliminated would be impoverished and constricted.

There are, of course, times in our lives when safety is vital.

We crave it for our children since they are not yet able to withstand the pressures and buffeting of life (though some might say that today we protect them too much). There are also other times – times of desolation and sorrow, times of depression or stress, times when we are physically ill or simply below par – when it is important to seek refuge and comfort until we are strong again. There are times of life, which for some people drag on year after bleak year, when we are already in a wilderness, a wilderness not of our choosing, which saps our strength, closes down our world, and brings the sharp pain of grief. These are not times to venture out into the wild spaces; these are times of waiting for healing and hope.

When we are well and strong, however, we can risk much more. At times like these, it is worth reminding ourselves of the quote by John A. Shedd in his collection *Salt from My Attic*: 'a ship in harbor is safe, but that is not what ships are built for'. This simple adage is rich with meaning. Our vocation as followers of Jesus is to live up to God's calling in our lives. Such a calling, as we will see again in the second half of this book, requires us to be prepared to lay down our lives, to take up our cross, and follow the one whose own path took him to suffering and death. We could stay safe in the harbour or we could unfurl our sails and sail out into the wideness of the sea, living up to our calling to be true followers of Christ whatever the risk or cost. Of course we should not take unnecessary and foolhardy risks but, like ships, human beings are intended to live in wide spaces – in our version of the open sea – where danger and salvation abide side by side.[1]

Such sentiments are reminiscent of the striking prayer often attributed to Sir Francis Drake:

---

1 I am fully aware of the irony of introducing the sea, which abounds with water, into a section about wilderness, which does not. Nevertheless, quantities of water aside, there are powerful overlaps between the two – both are places in which danger and salvation jostle side by side.

Disturb us, O Lord

>*when we are too well-pleased with ourselves*
>*when our dreams have come true because we*
>*dreamed too little, because we sailed too*
>*close to the shore.*

Disturb us, O Lord

>*when with the abundance of things we possess,*
>*we have lost our thirst for the water of life*
>*when, having fallen in love with time,*
>*we have ceased to dream of eternity*
>*and in our efforts to build a new earth,*
>*we have allowed our vision of Heaven to grow*
>*dim.*

Stir us, O Lord

>*to dare more boldly, to venture into wider seas*
>*where storms show Thy mastery,*
>*where losing sight of land, we shall find the*
>*stars.*

In the name of Him who pushed back the horizons
of our hopes
and invited the brave to follow.
Amen.

On journeying into the wilderness in lent

Lent can, if we let it, summon us from the safe harbours of our lives into a wide expanse of existence. Part of the point of deciding to lay things down or to take things up (depending on the decisions we make as Lent begins) is that in doing so we make our lives unfamiliar, even if only in a small way. We check ourselves as we reach for those familiar safety devices like chocolate or alcohol, and challenge ourselves into a less familiar response. We discomfort ourselves by choosing to do something we might otherwise not do and in so doing open the expanses of our lives in a different way.

One of the things that I try and do every year is to choose to do something that will place me right out of my comfort zone. It might be something that I do, or people that I go and speak to, or an event I might attend. In a sense it doesn't really matter what it is but I try and do it at least once a year, if not more often. This is not some odd form of masochism but a genuine attempt to broaden my horizons, to live courageously in the open spaces in the attempt to learn something new about myself, about others and about God. I don't always do it in Lent but I do strive to do it as often as I can, and Lent is always a good time to ask how well I have done on that front recently.

Each of the Christian seasons has its own flavour or characteristic. Each season offers us something to learn about waiting (Advent) or joy (Easter) or ordinariness and its importance (Ordinary time). In a way Lent is a more complex season as it offers us a range of characteristics to reflect on but, for me, one of its key flavours is spaciousness; a spaciousness that summons us to lift our eyes from the humdrum constriction of everyday existence; that invites us to strip our cluttered existences back to the bare minimum so that we can discern more fully what brings us life; that challenges us to look deep and hard at those things we try to avoid – and from them to learn who we really are.

What kind of wilderness?

The question we face during Lent is what wilderness experience we need to encounter this year. Of course few, if any, of us will spend Lent in an actual wilderness or desert. The challenge that Lent brings is the challenge of our willingness to enter an emotional or spiritual wilderness. This is not quite as 'grand' a challenge as that statement makes it sound. Entering the wilderness during Lent requires us deliberately to leave behind our known landscape; those patterns of behaviour and response that mark our lives as we know them. It dares us to lift our eyes beyond our humdrum lives and experiences to the God who awaits us in the wide place, and to see ourselves, God and the world in a new way.

In my experience each year Lent brings with it a different challenge to experience and from which to learn. Sometimes the message it holds out for us is gentle, a balm to the soul. Sometimes it is disturbing and unsettling. Sometimes it is uplifting and inspiring; sometimes bleak and unremitting. Each year is different. Each year we need to ask ourselves where the Spirit is driving us this year.

Lent can, if we aren't careful, turn into a spiritual strong man or strong woman competition: 'I have given up everything in my life that I enjoy, will pray for four hours a day, read 20 books and loftily look down on those poor mortals who can only give up chocolate for half of Lent'. It is an obvious thing to say but, like many obvious things, is worth saying anyway. Lent is not a competition. We do not become more spiritual the more miserable we are. There is no prize to be gained by outstripping others in our Lenten abstinence.

What we 'do' for Lent is far less important than who we become. We love to ask each other what we are giving up for Lent – I know I do – but a more important question is who are you becoming this Lent? What have you learnt about yourself and about God that is transforming you? It is a far more personal and much more relevant question, though not one we might choose to answer in public.

It may be that you neither give up anything nor take up anything, but find the spaciousness for your journey in another way. It might be that you give up exactly what you always do or find something new to try. It might be that you take up something new or stick with whatever you did last year. The 'what' is of little importance. The choice is between you and God. The key thing is discovering the spaciousness you need that will provide you with the opportunity to learn new lessons, to grow in faith, and to give God the chance to meet you in a new way.

Last year I gave up what I often give up in Lent – tea, coffee, chocolate and alcohol. I also gave up something new – social media. I found all of them taxing in different ways but none of them transformed my life quite in the way that following a very simple practice suggested in Pádraig Ó Tuama's wonderful book *In the Shelter: Finding a Home in the World* did. In this book, Pádraig suggests that rather than feeling the need to analyse, understand and comprehend every experience, hope and fear that we encounter we should greet them with a simple 'hello'. So last Lent, all Lent, that is what I did. I said hello to early mornings, which I hate. I said hello to the daffodils that broke into flower. I said hello to my fear about whether I would be able to continue to do the writing that I love. I said hello to the bubbling sense of spring as March drew on and to a couple of vicious reviews of me and my work. I said hello to some fun days out with my husband and children and to my father's terminal illness.

This 'saying hello' gave me the spaciousness I needed last Lent. I am someone whose constant inner conversation crowds out so much else: What should I think? What should I be feeling? What are they thinking and feeling? What have I done wrong? What could I do better? Who is going to criticize me next? My inner chatter is incessant and dull. The gift of the practice of simply greeting life as it was, and moving on, dampened the chatter and kept within me an open space. It took quite some reminding to learn that I didn't have to work out what I thought or felt about everything. I simply acknowledged their existence. What was transformative for me was that as I did so, a few times I felt the palpable, loving presence of God, standing with me, and greeting the world along with me.

That was the gift of last Lent. The question of what the gift of this Lent will be I cannot know yet – and I cannot even know if this Lent will bring a gift – but I am confident that, if it does bring a gift, the gift will come in ways I do not expect. The ambiguity of the wilderness means that we cannot know in advance what the wilderness experience will hold out for us this time but, good or bad, challenging or soothing, we can be confident that it will change us.

Jesus, the wilderness, and discipleship

As we will see in chapters 3–4 below, one of the themes that emerges from Jesus' own time in the wilderness is the theme of identity and calling. In the longer temptation narratives, the formula the devil asked two out of three times was 'If you are the Son of God, then …' Of course we already know that Jesus was, indeed, the Son of God. God declared him to be so at his baptism ('… a voice from heaven said, "This is my Son, the Beloved, with whom I am well pleased."', Matthew 3.17). The question for us, the readers, is not *whether* Jesus was the Son of God but *what kind of* Son of God he would choose to be.

Would he choose to be the kind of Son of God who took shortcuts, did things the easy way, gave reverence to those who clamoured for it and relied on this son-ship to get him out of difficulties, all for his own convenience and glory? Or would he be the kind of Son of God who took the long patient road, who put the needs of others above his own, who stayed true and faithful to his calling, all for the salvation of the world? We do, of course, know the answer to this question. We already know what kind of Son of God Jesus chose to be, not only through his life but at the moment of his death. One question, however, still rings through the centuries into our own ears. This question asks us about our own discipleship. What kind of disciple will you be? Will you take shortcuts, do things the easy way, give reverence to those who clamour for it and rely on discipleship for quick easy fixes to life's dilemmas? Or will you take the long patient road; a road that puts the needs of others above your own. Will you stay true and faithful to your calling for the sake of the one who called us to take up our cross and follow him? Lent allows us the time and the space to reflect on our everyday discipleship and what it asks of us.

Discipleship is a word that is often used but that can feel a little vague. What, precisely, does it mean to be a disciple of Jesus and how will we know if we are doing it 'right'? It is probably worth beginning an answer to this kind of question with the reassurance of the reminder of the disciples in Mark's Gospel. In Mark's Gospel, in particular, the disciples are a somewhat ramshackle group. Time and time again they seemed to get it wrong: they misunderstood what Jesus was talking about (Mark. 8.16); tried to dissuade Jesus from following his calling to suffering and death (Mark 8.33); asked for honours that simply didn't exist (Mark 10.37; fell asleep when he needed their companionship most (Mark. 14.37) and then deserted him entirely (Mark 14.50). If Mark is anything to go by we can't get it much more 'wrong' than the first disciples did. Yet 'wrong' as they got it, they remained Jesus' disciples.

Nevertheless, Mark's Gospel seems to be designed to inspire us to learn from their example both good and bad, and through this to grow in comprehension and faithfulness into the kind of disciples that Jesus might have had in mind. Mark's Gospel often feels as though it is inviting us, the readers, to ask ourselves the question of what being a disciple of Jesus requires of us. If we had been Peter, or James or John, how might we have responded to him? If we had been the women at the tomb, what might we have done in response to the command to 'go, tell' of Jesus' resurrection. The purpose of revealing the failings and weaknesses of the first disciples is not so that we can feel superior to them – they are after all the ones who took the good news of Jesus Christ, Son of God, to the ends of the earth – but so that we can ask ourselves the question of what kind of disciples Jesus might have hoped for and what we might need to do to live up to his calling of us.

This is a theme to which we will return in the second half of the book, but for now it is worth introducing it a little. A natural answer to the question of 'what a disciple is' is that a disciple is a follower of Jesus. This answer is not wrong; it is just not entirely right. The first disciples are characterized by the fact that they responded to Jesus' call to 'come, follow me': Simon Peter and Andrew followed him by the Sea of Galilee (Matthew 4.19; Mark 1.17); Matthew/Levi the tax collector left his tax booth and followed him (Matthew 9.9; Luke 5.27); Philip followed him after going to find Nathanael (John 1.43). The disciples did follow Jesus but this is not what the word 'disciple' meant.

The Greek word *mathētēs* and its Latin companion (*discipulus*, from which we get our English word 'disciple') both mean 'a learner'. Indeed this was the point of the disciples' following. They followed Jesus so that they could learn from him: they listened to his teaching, asked questions, got things wrong, watched him heal people, asked him more questions, got more things wrong, ate with him, observed his conflicts with the leaders of his day, and as they followed they learned. They learned who Jesus was and who they were. Following was what enabled them to learn; learning was what made them disciples.

It is a small but vital change of perspective. If we think of being disciples solely as following Jesus, then the expectation of transformation becomes less important. Whereas learning requires us to change and change and change so that the question becomes what are you learning now from Jesus? What did you learn last week? What will you learn next week? The uncomfortable question this raises for us all is whether our learning is, indeed, on-going, or whether we are relying on learning we did five, ten or more years ago. Can our Christian communities genuinely be described as vibrant places of learning from and about Jesus?

Rabbis and disciples

It is important not to mix up the world of Jesus' day with what developed later. Rabbinic Judaism in its fullest form grew up after the fall of the temple in Jerusalem in AD 70. With Rabbinic Judaism there developed a careful method of teaching which culminated in the brightest of students becoming a *talmid* (or expert learner) with one of the greatest Rabbis, and then in their turn becoming a Rabbi themselves. This system was not in place during the time of Jesus. Nevertheless, we do know that a number of people were called Rabbis at this stage and that certain people learnt from them. For example, the New Testament tells us that the apostle Paul was said to have learned from the great Rabbi Gamaliel (Acts 22.3), and other external sources like Josephus and the Mishnah also make extensive references to Rabbis and their disciples.

In some ways being a disciple of Jesus was no different from being a disciple of any other Rabbi. While the learning that took place would have involved 'knowledge transfer', far more important in the Rabbi–disciple relationship was imprinting on the disciple the master's way of seeing the world. Good disciples would learn to see the world around them through the eyes of the Rabbi. All the way through the Gospels, we can see this happening with Jesus and his disciples. Time and time again Jesus showed the disciples the way of compassion and love; of humility and sacrifice, and of endurance and hope.

It is all too easy to mix up teaching and learning. It is nice to imagine that when you teach someone something, they learn. There is undoubtedly a connection between teaching and learning, particularly between good teaching and effective learning, but any teacher will tell you that what people learn can be very different from what you intended to teach them. I have been variously irritated and amused by the modern Higher Education's obsession with learning outcomes. Learning outcomes are defined as a statement of what a student will learn in the session you are about to teach. I always want to say that I can tell you my 'teaching goals', but not the students, 'learning outcomes'. In over 20 years of teaching, I have discovered that the very best sessions – those from which people go away inspired and transformed – all have one thing in common: that people learned from them far more than I dreamed that they could. The best learning is gloriously unpredictable. People can make such great leaps of creativity and imagination that what they learn far outstrips what they have been taught.

This is because learning is not just about facts and knowledge. It is about understanding, insight and vision. The Rabbi–disciple relationship understood this. The disciples did not just learn from Jesus' teaching, like that in the Sermon on the Mount. They learnt from being with him: asking questions, getting things wrong and watching him interact with others. They learnt from what he did as much as from what he said. This has a great deal to teach us about discipleship in our own communities.

In many churches today discipleship is, fascinatingly, often associated with two things: new Christians and courses. Most 'discipleship courses' are aimed at people new to the faith who come to a course to be taught the fundamentals of Christian life and belief. Don't get me wrong, I'm a big fan of these. However, if we think that by running a discipleship course one or more times a year we have discipleship completely in hand, we miss the point catastrophically. One tiny aspect of discipleship is teaching knowledge to new Christians, but it is only one tiny aspect.

Discipleship is for all Christians, whether they have been a disciple for 5 minutes or 50 years. For our communities to be discipleship communities they need to be places vibrant with learning; places of questioning and discussion; places of listening and comprehension; places in which we learn from Jesus in as many ways as possible. It is very important for new Christians to learn about the faith, but why should they if they don't see the rest of us learning too? Learning is not just for new Christians, it is for anyone who seeks to be a disciple of Jesus. Learning is to disciples what breathing is to human beings.

I have, for a while, been haunted by a question that someone asked me a few years ago. She was newly appointed to a post and her role was overseeing the learning of a certain Christian community. She was an expert trainer and had worked extensively in business, education and health care. She had thought her job to be quite straightforward, using her training skills in a Christian context, but had found the role almost undoable. Driven to distraction by a profound reluctance on behalf of many to learn, she exclaimed in frustration: 'I don't understand, isn't the Church a learning environment?' Her question is a fearsome one. If we are driven to answer 'no', then we are really saying that we are not communities of disciples, and that, to me, feels a terrifying thing to admit.

So what might we learn about discipleship from Jesus and his disciples? The first and most important lesson must surely be that we are called to be disciples of Jesus, not of anyone else. Hard as the first disciples found it, they had an easier task than we do. They learnt by spending time with Jesus. Our task is to find ways to do this today. What this looks like for each one of us will be different, and sometimes it can take a lifetime to discover what 'spending time with Jesus Christ' can mean in practice. The problem is that we all too easily look to 'tasks'. If we pray, go to church, read the Bible, and 'do good things', then it is tempting to declare that we have done all that is required. The problem is that it is possible to do all of those things and not really to have spent time in the presence of Jesus. Being a disciple is more about spending time in the presence of Jesus, and learning to see the world as he sees it, than it is about checking off a 'to-do' list.

The other key lesson seems to me to be that learning takes many different forms. We need to be on constant look-out for ways in which we, ourselves, might learn or might help others to learn. Learning happens in friendship and conversation and in formal teaching and listening; it happens when we ask questions and when we hear other people's answers; it happens in large crowds and small mentoring contexts; it happens when we eat together or fast together; it happens when we pray or sing. The call to discipleship is a call on the whole of our lives. A community of disciples is one that learns together in many different ways. Teaching is one element, but only one element, of the learning that can take place. Our goal is to find ways, as many as possible, to learn with our gaze ever on the Jesus from whom we learn. We will be most successful when we craft communities that simply enjoy spending time together and in the presence of Jesus – then we will truly be discipleship communities.

There are far more lessons about discipleship to learn than these two, but they are a good place to begin and we will reflect on more as the book unfolds. One of the many values of Lent is that it drives us back year after year to the question of discipleship, asking us to reflect again on our own learning from Jesus. What are we learning from Jesus today? This week? This month? This Lent? This year? As we take the time to enter the wilderness – whatever form this takes for us – it gives us the time and the space to reflect on this question afresh.

Let me go there

In each of the books in this series I have chosen a poem by R. S. Thomas which, in whole or in part, to my mind at least, encapsulates the key themes of the season. The poems are suggested as additional food for thought, as companions on the way through the season, offering an additional way of looking at the key themes. 'The Coming' is in many ways perfect for Lent. With Thomas's characteristically sparse language, he suggests to us a world in great need of the love and recreation that only God could bring. He paints a picture of the desperation of the world and the bleakness of the task set before the Son.

Here the Son looked long and hard at the wilderness that lay before him; the wilderness was not of a single place – such as he visited during the temptations – but of the whole world: a wilderness that cried out for love in the midst of its pain and despair. At the end of the poem the Son said, as we knew he always would, 'Let me go there'. He knew the enormity of the task that lay before him, he understood fully the ambiguity that the wilderness always represented, he appreciated the depth of the despair laid out before him – and still he chose to go.

This is what we remember in Lent. Jesus' life and ministry is summed up by the choices he made in the wilderness when he was tempted by the devil. He could have chosen the easy way but instead he chose the hard way. He could have chosen the way that brought personal honour and praise, but instead chose the way that brought love and compassion. He could have chosen grandeur and comfort, but instead chose to live alongside those who had nothing. He saw and knew exactly what he chose … but still he said 'Let me go there'.

This is the Rabbi we follow, the master from whom we learn. This Lent may we hear the challenge again to come, follow him. We know what it will ask of us. We know the cost that it will bring. The question is whether we, like him, can echo those words 'Let me go there'.

The Coming

And God held in his hand
A small globe. Look he said.
The son looked. Far off,
As through water, he saw
A scorched land of fierce
Colour. The light burned
There; crusted buildings
Cast their shadows: a bright
Serpent, A river
Uncoiled itself, radiant
With slime.
On a bare
Hill a bare tree saddened
The sky. Many People
Held out their thin arms
To it, as though waiting
For a vanished April
To return to its crossed
Boughs. The son watched
Them. Let me go there, he said.

R. S. Thomas

1

The Wilderness ...
Desolation and Redemption

In the introduction I noted the ambiguity of the wilderness in the Old Testament: the idea that the wilderness is a place both of terror and of shelter; of death and of redemption; of despair and of hope. In this chapter we begin to explore this idea a little more so that when, in the subsequent three chapters, we turn our attention to Jesus' temptations in the wilderness, the backdrop to those stories will begin to look more familiar and the resonance of Jesus going into the wilderness will be easier to discern.

For obvious reasons we cannot look at all the references to the wilderness in the Bible – that would take far too long. Instead I have chosen six of, what are for me, the most powerful passages that encapsulate the essence of the wilderness in the Old Testament. Although we spend this chapter with one eye on what the wilderness meant for the biblical writers, we need to focus the other eye on what counts as wilderness for us today. The power of the wilderness as a metaphor is found in its breadth of usage. It is certainly a place, but it can evoke other experiences too. It can suggest an emotion, a relationship, a job, a time of life (to mention just a few examples). The emotional resonance of the wilderness is as powerful today as it ever was; our task is to learn to recognize it when it occurs and to live in expectation that the God who met Hagar, Moses, Elijah and others in the wilderness may meet us there too.

Exploring the wilderness also challenges us to remember and pray for those whose lives, like Hagar, have been turned upside down and have been destroyed so thoroughly that, like her, their best and most life-giving choice is to flee into the desolation of the wilderness.

1

Genesis 16.6–13 Then Sarai dealt harshly with her, and she ran away from her. The angel of the LORD found her by a spring of water in the wilderness, the spring on the way to Shur. And he said, 'Hagar, slave-girl of Sarai, where have you come from and where are you going?' … So she named the LORD who spoke to her, 'You are El-roi'; for she said, 'Have I really seen God and remained alive after seeing him?'

Genesis 21.14–16 So Abraham rose early in the morning, and took bread and a skin of water, and gave it to Hagar, putting it on her shoulder, along with the child, and sent her away. And she departed, and wandered about in the wilderness of Beer-sheba. When the water in the skin was gone, she cast the child under one of the bushes. Then she went and sat down opposite him a good way off, about the distance of a bowshot; for she said, 'Do not let me look on the death of the child.' …

*To read the whole story read **Genesis 16.1–16** and then **Genesis 21.1–20***

If there is a story that is iconic in its portrayal of the profound ambiguity of the wilderness, it would need to be the story of Hagar which is woven throughout the larger narrative of God's promise to Abraham and Sarah. In fact, it is the flip side of that story. In Genesis 12.1–3, and then again in Genesis 15.1–5, God promised Abraham that he would be the father of a great nation (12.2) and that his descendants would be as many as the stars (15.5). The only problem was that Abraham and Sarah had no children at all.

So at the start of chapter 16, Abraham and Sarah began to look for their own solution to the problem. In all fairness, they had waited a long time – a very long time. Genesis 16.3 notes that they had waited for ten years for a child to be born. Nevertheless, in Genesis 16 they decided to look for their own solution – someone to bear a child for them – and somewhat inevitably this ended up in tension, jealousy and dispute.

The two stories in chapters 16 and 21 mirror each other. In both Hagar ended up in the wilderness. The first time she ran away; the second she was driven away. The first time she was pregnant with Ishmael; the second she took him with her. In Genesis 16, there is little description of the terror she found there, but in Genesis 21 its full horror comes to the fore. In Genesis 21, Hagar clearly believed that she and her baby – Ishmael – were going to die, so she abandoned him under a bush so that she didn't have to put herself through the horror of seeing it happen. In Genesis 21 we are left in no doubt of the terror of the wilderness. Hagar believed that in the wilderness she and her son would meet their end.

The theme that lies at the heart of these stories is probably summed up best with Hagar's words in Genesis 16.13 ('You are El-roi'; for she said, 'Have I really seen God and remained alive after seeing him?'). As with many important verses, this is very hard to phrase well in English. What the Hebrew says is more complex than is contained here. It is something along the lines of 'You are the God of seeing [*El-roi*] because she said "have I also seen after my seer?"' This could have a range of meanings but it probably means that Hagar recognized that the one who sees her had appeared to her.

It is this theme of the 'God of seeing' that is important here. Hagar, an outsider in this story, was cast off by Abraham and Sarah, sent into the wilderness and left to die, because she no longer fitted in with their plan. But the 'God of seeing' did not cast her off. He saw her, he heard the cry of her son (21.17), and appeared so that she, in her turn, could see and hear the one who saw and heard her. In the midst of the wilderness Hagar was 'seen' in a way she was never seen in her normal life. In the midst of her desolation God appeared so that she could know that she was truly seen and truly loved. The God of seeing remains the same today and in our wildernesses still sees and hears us even when we feel that no one else does.

2

Exodus 15.22–24 and 16.2–3 Then Moses ordered Israel to set out from the Red Sea, and they went into the wilderness of Shur. They went for three days in the wilderness and found no water. When they came to Marah, they could not drink the water of Marah because it was bitter. That is why it was called Marah. And the people complained against Moses, saying, 'What shall we drink?'… The whole congregation of the Israelites complained against Moses and Aaron in the wilderness. The Israelites said to them, 'If only we had died by the hand of the LORD in the land of Egypt, when we sat by the fleshpots and ate our fill of bread; for you have brought us out into this wilderness to kill this whole assembly with hunger.'

People enter the wilderness for all sorts of reasons. Some have no choice; others choose the wilderness as the most life-giving place they can find. Some go to die; others to rest and recover. We see this in the biblical tradition itself. The wilderness represents very different experiences for those who fled Egypt with Moses, than for Hagar. Hagar was driven into the wilderness to die, whereas the people of God escaped to the wilderness to find freedom.

The story of escape from slavery in Egypt through the Red Sea is one of the essential narratives of the Old Testament. It speaks of freedom from oppression, of faith and of new life. It tells of a God who will always free people from slavery. Indeed so powerful is this story of freedom that, through the ages, oppressed people from around the world have looked to it for inspiration and hope. It is striking to notice, therefore, that those least inspired by their escape from slavery were God's people themselves.

Barely had they left Egypt and crossed the Red Sea than they wished that they hadn't left at all. As we see in Exodus 15 and 16, almost straightaway they began to wish that they were back in the 'safety' of slavery. There are times when the wilderness represents a freedom that is too frightening for us to accept. At least in Egypt God's people had food to eat and water to drink, even if their overlords beat them to death as well.

What is going on in Exodus 15—16 is a powerful but natural human reaction. You can set people's bodies free, but it takes much longer to free their minds. People who experience oppression over a long period of time find in it an odd level of safety alongside the brutality. They get used to it and can look back on it with a kind of nostalgia once the immediate danger is past. The freedom of the wilderness can, sometimes, be too much after the confines of oppression. People who have learnt to be passive year after year struggle with being active when freedom comes their way.

Of course, God's people were right to fear the wilderness. It is a vast, unfriendly expanse where many easily die of hunger and thirst. What they had forgotten, however, is that they hadn't gone there alone. The God who had freed them from slavery in the first place went with them, showing them the way, providing manna and water when they needed it most.

Their bodies were free but it took a long time for their minds to catch up. The problem with freedom is that it is insecure, unknown and can be terrifying. It took God's people a very long time – maybe even longer than the forty years they had to wander in the wilderness – to realize that the only way to navigate the freedom of the wilderness is with their hand in the hand of God. It is precisely the ambiguous nature of the wilderness that means that it is at one and the same time a place of freedom and hope and a place of danger and despair. The difference between each experience is the presence of God. Only when we trust in the one who is entirely worthy of that trust can the wilderness become a place of joyful freedom rather than terrifying danger. The wilderness does not change but our reaction to it can.

3

1 Kings 19.1–8 *Ahab told Jezebel all that Elijah had done, and how he had killed all the prophets with the sword. Then Jezebel sent a messenger to Elijah, saying, 'So may the gods do to me, and more also, if I do not make your life like the life of one of them by this time tomorrow.' Then he was afraid; he got up and fled for his life, and came to Beersheba, which belongs to Judah; he left his servant there. But he himself went a day's journey into the wilderness, and came and sat down under a solitary broom tree. He asked that he might die: 'It is enough; now, O LORD, take away my life, for I am no better than my ancestors.' Then he lay*

down under the broom tree and fell asleep. Suddenly an
angel touched him and said to him, 'Get up and eat.' He
looked, and there at his head was a cake baked on hot
stones, and a jar of water. He ate and drank, and lay down
again. The angel of the LORD came a second time, touched
him, and said, 'Get up and eat, otherwise the journey will
be too much for you.' He got up, and ate and drank; then
he went in the strength of that food for forty days and forty
nights to Horeb the mount of God.

The story of Elijah fleeing for his life into the desert continues
our theme of the wilderness well. Here the physical wilderness mirrors Elijah's emotional wilderness (as indeed it did
for Hagar in Genesis 16 and 21). If you are alert you will
notice that Elijah was in the same desert as Hagar – the
wilderness of Beer-sheba, which is the northern part of the
Negeb desert; Mount Horeb (otherwise known as Mount
Sinai) is in the southern part of this same desert.

This story follows on immediately from Elijah's famous
battle with the prophets of Baal. There Elijah triumphed
spectacularly and, as so often happens after great effort (and
success), he fell into a pit of despair and wanted to die. In
fairness, this would not have been helped by knowing that
Jezebel wanted to kill him, but it is fascinating to note that
his desire to die would have given her exactly what she
wanted. He had defeated himself before ever Jezebel's messenger had even approached him. So, as I observed above,
Elijah didn't just flee into the physical desert – he entered
an emotional desert too.

What is particularly interesting in this story is how God
responded to Elijah in 'his wilderness'. I might have been
tempted to tell Elijah to get a grip, to recognize the significance of what he had achieved and to go back and face
Jezebel in her wrath – but that would have been the wrong
thing to do. There are times, as with Hagar, when people

have no choice but to flee into the wilderness for their own safety; there are other times, as with the Israelites leaving Egypt, when entry into the wilderness brings freedom, and there are yet other times, as here, when the wilderness offers space to rest and recover before returning to face what we are called to do once more.

God's response to Elijah, via an angel, is breathtakingly simple: to let him sleep (19.5–6) and to feed him (19.5 and 19.7). We might have expected a more sophisticated response but the reality was that Elijah was physically and emotionally exhausted and he needed time to rest and recover. Times in which we experience an emotional wilderness, such as Elijah encounters here, can sometimes seduce us into believing that only the most complex of solutions can help, when the reality is that sleep, food and time-out go a long way towards providing the help we need.

Elijah entered the wilderness for the wrong reason – he fled somewhere bleak so he could die miserably in peace – but it turned out that he had unwittingly gone to exactly the right place. The wilderness gave him solitude and spaciousness in which to recover and the angel gave him sleep and the nourishment to mend his exhausted body. Then, and only then, did God appear to Elijah on the top of Mount Horeb/Sinai in the sound of sheer silence (to quote the NRSV) or with a still small voice of calm (to use Charles Wesley's phrase from the hymn 'O Lord and Father of Mankind'). Before he had rested and recovered Elijah would simply not have been able to encounter God in any meaningful way.

There is much to learn from this. I meet many exhausted Christians who very quickly fall to complaining that God feels distant or out of reach. While it is entirely possible that the reasons for this are many and varied, it is surely worth checking, first, whether what we need most is simply space in which to recover, sleep and eat a hearty meal.

Lent can be a very busy time but a good Lenten exercise might be to spend some 'Elijah time'. Most of us cannot take the whole of Lent (the amount of time it took Elijah to travel from Beer-sheba to Mount Horeb, 1 Kings 19.8) for this, but a day or two might just be the 'Lenten discipline' we need so that we can return refreshed and renewed, ready once more to do what we have been called to do.

4

Psalm 107.1–7 O give thanks to the LORD, for he is good; for his steadfast love endures for ever. Let the redeemed of the LORD say so, those he redeemed from trouble and gathered in from the lands, from the east and from the west, from the north and from the south. Some wandered in desert wastes², finding no way to an inhabited town; hungry and thirsty, their soul fainted within them. Then they cried to the LORD in their trouble, and he delivered them from their distress; he led them by a straight way, until they reached an inhabited town.

One of the striking features of the way in which the biblical writers talked about God is that they described God's character in terms of what he had done. God was the God who freed his people from slavery, who brought them into the Promised Land, who saved them from their enemies, etc. The list is a long one and the Psalms, in particular, provide a large number of the deeds that tell us about the character of God. This does not end in the Old Testament, as the New Testament writers continued to describe God by his action – most particularly his action of raising Jesus from the dead.

If read in the wrong way, this way of describing God can <u>feel backward looking</u>: urging us to forget what is going on

2 Literally 'in the wilderness, in a wasteland'.

today and look back in reminiscence to the good old days and how things used to be. Of course it is all too easy to fall into the trap of a rose-tinted nostalgia that uproots us from the present and locks us unhelpfully in how things used to be, but this is not what is meant by this kind of description.

This becomes clear in Psalms like Psalm 107 with its refrain that runs throughout it: 'O give thanks to the LORD, for he is good; for his steadfast love endures for ever'. Psalm 107 does contain a catalogue of what God has done but it is a catalogue designed to teach us about the character of God. If God has saved people in the past we can be confident that he will do so again and again … because he is good and his steadfast love endures forever. We rehearse God's deeds in the past not to lock us into history but to lift our eyes from our current despair in hope, and to give us confidence that this God will act in the same way again.

As we reflect on the wilderness tradition we see that the God in whom we believe is a God who intervenes in the wilderness. He intervened for Hagar when she and Ishmael were on the point of death. He intervened for those in this Psalm whose soul (or life) fainted within them. And he will do so again.

It is worth noting that another refrain also runs through this Psalm: 'Then they cried to the LORD in their trouble, and he delivered them from their distress'. It occurs in verses 6, 13, 19 and 28. God did save his people … after they cried to him. Just like Hagar in the previous passage, God does hear our cry – but we need to cry it first. It is very easy in hard times to curl up and whimper quietly to ourselves or to feel that we are too angry or too miserable to address God. Even the briefest readings of the Psalms indicates that there is no such thing as too angry or too miserable to speak to God. God wants us to cry to him from whatever wilderness we find ourselves in – what we say (however rude it might be) is up to us.

Of course this raises the question of what happens when God does not appear to hear or to answer. It is not a simple question, nor is there an easy answer to give. It is, nevertheless, worth reminding ourselves that God is neither a slot machine nor a fairy godmother. God hears our cries as God hears them, not as we dictate. God also hears our cries to his timetable, not to ours. It is striking simply to notice the length of time that people waited for God even in the Bible (Abraham and Sarah, for example, appear to have waited over 25 years for the fulfilment of God's promise to them – another 15 years after the ten they had waited in Genesis 16). It may just be that when we have decided that God has not heard us he has, and has either responded in a way we do not expect or will do so in the future. This may be no more comfort to us than it was to the biblical characters but is, nevertheless, worth bearing in mind.

As the Psalmist declares in Psalm 107 God does intervene in our times in the wilderness. God does hear our cry. The first step towards this is to cry out in the first place.

5

Jeremiah 31.1–5 At that time, says the LORD, I will be the God of all the families of Israel, and they shall be my people. Thus says the LORD: The people who survived the sword found grace in the wilderness; when Israel sought for rest, the LORD appeared to him from far away. I have loved you with an everlasting love; therefore I have continued my faithfulness to you. Again I will build you, and you shall be built, O virgin Israel! Again you shall take your tambourines, and go forth in the dance of the merrymakers. Again you shall plant vineyards on the mountains of Samaria; the planters shall plant, and shall enjoy the fruit.

In this chapter we have been tracing the power of 'the wilderness' in the imagination of the Old Testament writers. Although each one of the events we have looked at contributes to the significance of the image – Hagar's fleeing from Abraham and Sarah; the escape of Moses and the people of God from Egypt, and Elijah's need for recuperation after battling the prophets of Baal – it is, of course, the wilderness wandering, after fleeing slavery in Egypt and before settling in the Promised Land, that lays the foundation of the importance of the wilderness. Many passages – including Psalm 107 and this passage from Jeremiah – refer back to the Exodus experience as symbolic of God's whole relationship with his people.

Just as in Psalm 107, so here in Jeremiah 31.1–5 the wilderness wandering is used as assurance of hope for the future. The importance of this particular passage is that, in it, we can begin to see where the Old Testament writers' ambiguous relationship with the wilderness came from. The wilderness was indeed desolate and terrifying. What God's people should have found in the wilderness was death and despair but instead they found grace – God's overwhelming and undeserved generosity.

It was not the wilderness itself that was ambiguous; God's presence made it so. The life-giving, hope-bringing, loving presence of God brought grace into the desolate plains of the wilderness. Where God was, the wilderness was a wilderness no more. As Isaiah said, where God was present rivers sprang forth in the desert and desolate places became rich and fertile (Isaiah 43.19–20). The message of hope in Jeremiah is based entirely on this vision of God's presence. God's people had found grace in the wilderness rather than death and this is what transformed the place from death to life; from despair to hope.

The key element of this Jeremiah passage can be found in verse 3. God's people found grace instead of death in the wilderness because God loved them with an everlasting love and continued his faithfulness to them. The word translated 'faithfulness' is the central covenant word that was also used in the refrain of Psalm 107: 'his steadfast love endures for ever'. The variation in translation illustrates quite how hard it is to translate the Hebrew word *hesed* into English. The word has a broad range of meanings from loyalty and faithfulness, through to goodness and kindness, to steadfast love. In short it sums up the nature of God – God's steadfastness, loyalty, faithfulness, goodness, kindness and love towards his people.

This is the content of Jeremiah's message of hope here. The God whose love and faithfulness knew no bounds would be present with the people he was talking to in exactly the same way that he had been with Moses and the people of the Exodus. Just as they had found grace in the wilderness, so Jeremiah's audience could also find grace. At that point they would be rebuilt, they would dance with tambourines, and enjoy the fruit of vines.

This message does not end with Jeremiah's audience, any more than it ended with Moses and God's people in the wilderness. That is the point of the message. The God of steadfast love remains the same. God's presence in the wilderness – whatever form that wilderness takes – still provides grace, hope and steadfast love. Where God is, the wilderness loses its terrible grip in the face of overwhelming grace. When we find ourselves in an emotional wilderness – either individually or as a community or nation – the temptation is to hunker down as despair sweeps over us. Jeremiah's message here reminds us to look up, to wait expectantly for the God who has, since the dawn of time, transformed chaos into creation, the empty void into joyous hope.

God's people have always found grace in the midst of the wilderness ... there is no reason for this to stop now.

6

Isaiah 40.1–5 Comfort, O comfort my people, says your God. Speak tenderly to Jerusalem, and cry to her that she has served her term, that her penalty is paid, that she has received from the LORD's hand double for all her sins. A voice cries out: 'In the wilderness prepare the way of the LORD, make straight in the desert a highway for our God. Every valley shall be lifted up, and every mountain and hill be made low; the uneven ground shall become level, and the rough places a plain. Then the glory of the LORD shall be revealed, and all people shall see it together, for the mouth of the LORD has spoken.'

Our final 'wilderness' passage – the one picked up by the Gospel writers at the start of Jesus' ministry – to a certain extent completes our picture of the wilderness. Many of the passages about the wilderness that we have looked at tell the story of people who had no choice but to enter the wilderness. Hagar was driven there; Moses and the people fled there to escape slavery; Elijah also fled there in fear for his life. Each of them was found there by God and, as Jeremiah so beautifully put it, found grace.

This is the only passage of the six that suggests that entering the wilderness can be a choice. Here Isaiah challenges God's people not just to stumble on grace as they flee into the wilderness for another reason, but to go looking for it and to prepare for it.

The imagery chimes in strongly with the book of Ezekiel. Ezekiel 10 tells poignantly of God leaving the temple in Jerusalem just before the Babylonians destroyed it in the sixth century BC. The image he used there was of the glory of God leaving the temple on a chariot of cherubim. The message in Isaiah 40 seems to provide the ending to this image: God's people were to go out into the wilderness and prepare a way for God's return, the ground was to be levelled and a straight path fashioned to enable God's chariot – and hence his glorious presence – to return to his people once more.

In other words, Isaiah's audience was challenged so to believe that they would encounter God in the wilderness, that they were to go there on purpose – not driven by anything other than hope – and to prepare for the return of God when they could see no evidence of his presence in advance. Isaiah's message was one of reckless, joyous faith in the God who met his people in the wilderness. It is one thing to trust, as the Psalmist and Jeremiah suggest, that the God of steadfast love would come to find his people whenever they are driven into the wilderness; it is quite another to go there on purpose to prepare for God's return.

This is what Isaiah called God's people to do here and it is what John the Baptist did at the start of the Gospels. This was why it was so important that John the Baptist was to be found in the wilderness. It is why it was so important that Jesus began his ministry in the wilderness too. There, at long last, someone had heard the message and gone out to prepare the way for God's return. There, at long last, God returned as he had promised to do. It is tempting to be passive in relationship to the wilderness. Many of us at different times in our lives are driven there without any choice. The wisest and bravest of us, at those times, remember to hold on and wait for God's loving presence to come out to find us. But how many of us are valiant enough to journey there deliberately to prepare and wait for God's grace?

You might, with entire justification, be wondering what this would look like in practice. The answer, in my view, is that the wilderness represents all those occasions, places and events that we naturally shy away from because it feels as though they are barren, conflict-riven or hopeless; whether these be a hard conversation that needs to be had; a conflict that needs facing with compassion and generosity; something we should do which makes us want to shrivel up inside; or a political battle that must be fought. Isaiah's message seems to me to challenge us to journey into these situations courageously and in hopeful expectation of God's presence. This is not a call to masochism nor an invitation to choose to do something simply because it will make us miserable, but it is a call to courageous hope in the face of despair. It is a challenge to each one of us to stand firm in situations we might prefer to avoid, to light candles in the darkness wherever and whenever despair threatens to take hold, and rebelliously to expect and so proclaim God's presence in the most God-forsaken of situations and places.

As we have observed, the wilderness was a place of ambiguity simply because in the midst of desolation time and time again God met his people there. The wilderness itself never changed. It was a bleak, barren place in which death, hunger and despair lurked. What transformed it was the presence of God. Where God was, the wilderness became a place of oasis, of rest and refreshment. Where God was, there was grace. The message of the Old Testament was that the God who never changed was the God who over and over again met people in the wilderness and will continue to do so.

Perhaps most important of all, God calls us to choose to go out from our places of comfort into the wilderness – to those painful places of conflict, despair and hopelessness – and in them courageously to prepare for God's presence.

Lent is a season in which we are all called to be prophets, carrying the light of God's steadfast love into the most bleak places of wilderness and there proclaiming, as Isaiah urged in 40.9, 'here is your God'.

Questions for discussion and reflection

Reflecting on Scripture

Either:

- Discuss the passages from this chapter. Did any of the wilderness passages in this chapter speak to you more profoundly than the others? What was it about that passage that you related to most strongly?

- Decide as a group which of the passages you would like to read together as a group (it could either be the one that most people liked or alternatively the one you all least liked). Spend time reading it together and reflecting on what you hear from it this time.

Or:

- Read all the passages – it won't take very long – with each person in the group taking turns in reading out loud.

- Reflect together on what you learnt from hearing them all together. Did themes emerge? Did any one of them not fit with the others?

Discuss

The wilderness

- Have you ever been to an actual place that might be described as a wilderness? What kinds of emotions did you experience there?

- What kinds of experiences do we have today that might be described as 'a wilderness? (These might be personal experiences or could be things that have happened in the news here or overseas; they could be everyday experiences or something you have seen happening in your church.)

- If God were to bring redemption into these experiences of wilderness, what might we see happening?
- What is helpful about using the image of the wilderness to talk about our lives? And what is unhelpful?

The struggle of the wilderness

- If you know each other well enough you might want to share some experiences you have had of the struggle of the wilderness. If we understand wilderness as an emotional desert, then it might be helpful to share experiences of times when people in your group have experienced this and what they have learnt from this.

  (Only do this question if you are confident that your group can handle it!)

- Imagine that someone were to say something like 'I've been in a wilderness for a very long time and God has brought no redemption'. What would you say to them?

Going into the wilderness

- If, as Isaiah suggests, sometimes we need deliberately to go out into the wilderness to prepare for God, have you any ideas about what that might mean in practice?

ON RECOGNITION

Jesus and the wilderness in Mark

Mark's account of Jesus' temptation in the wilderness is very short. In fact, it is so short that it only warrants the title 'temptation narrative' when we read it through the lens of Matthew and Luke's Gospels. In Mark's account all we have is the bare bones of an account: Jesus was driven into the wilderness where he was tempted by Satan, was with the wild beasts, and was waited on by angels. Here the only connection between Jesus and Satan is that simple phrase: 'he was tempted by Satan'. There was no conversation between them; no challenge and response; no report of temptations successfully resisted.

What there is instead is a story entirely located in the wilderness. The wilderness narrative begins in Mark, ten or so verses earlier, when John the Baptist appeared there. This focus on the wilderness does not change until after verse 13 when the scene changes to Galilee and the start of Jesus' ministry proper. After John appeared in the wilderness, the people went out to it from Jerusalem and Judea; Jesus was baptized in the wilderness and then was driven further into it by the Spirit for forty days. In Mark, the wilderness provides the backdrop for our first encounter not only with John the Baptist but also with Jesus, and hints, as strongly as it is possible to do, that the redemption so long awaited was finally on its way. The question was whether anyone would notice.

The reflections in this section will all weave around Mark 1.2–13; you may want to read the whole passage through before you begin.

Mark 1.2–13 *As it is written in the prophet Isaiah, 'See, I am sending my messenger ahead of you, who will prepare your way; the voice of one crying out in the wilderness: "Prepare the way of the Lord, make his paths straight,"', John the baptizer appeared in the wilderness, proclaiming a baptism of repentance for the forgiveness of sins. And people from the whole Judean countryside and all the people of Jerusalem were going out to him, and were baptized by him in the river Jordan, confessing their sins. Now John was clothed with camel's hair, with a leather belt around his waist, and he ate locusts and wild honey. He proclaimed, 'The one who is more powerful than I is coming after me; I am not worthy to stoop down and untie the thong of his sandals. I have baptized you with water; but he will baptize you with the Holy Spirit.' In those days Jesus came from Nazareth of Galilee and was baptized by John in the Jordan. And just as he was coming up out of the water, he saw the heavens torn apart and the Spirit descending like a dove on him. And a voice came from heaven, 'You are my Son, the Beloved; with you I am well pleased.' And the Spirit immediately drove him out into the wilderness. He was in the wilderness for forty days, tempted by Satan; and he was with the wild beasts; and the angels waited on him.*

7

Mark 1.2 *As it is written in the prophet Isaiah, 'See, I am sending my messenger ahead of you, who will prepare your way'*

Malachi 3.1 and 4.5 *See, I am sending my messenger to prepare the way before me, and the Lord whom you seek will suddenly come to his temple. The messenger of the covenant in whom you delight – indeed, he is coming, says the* LORD *of hosts … Lo, I will send you the prophet Elijah before the great and terrible day of the* LORD *comes.*

The opening of Mark's Gospel begins exactly where the Old Testament ended. It invites us to imagine turning the page – or more accurately to unroll the scroll a little further – and to read on, with barely a break in between. Each of the Gospels in their own way remind us that the story they summon us to hear is not a new story that has dropped from the heavens hermetically sealed. It is an old, old story. It is the story of God's people. It is the story of God's love and constant attempts to mend their fractured relationship. Mark's way of reminding us of the ancient roots of his story is to pick up where Malachi left off.

The book of Malachi ended with the promise that God would send a messenger before him to prepare the people to receive their God. This messenger, the new Elijah, would make them ready for when God came to his people as he had promised he would. The only question was when would he come? How long did they have to wait for God to come to them? The opening to Mark's Gospel gives a loud and clear answer to this question. Barely had the beginning of the good news of Jesus Christ been announced (1.1) when this very messenger crashed into view.

Here the name of the messenger was John the baptizer but there is no doubt that, in Mark's mind, this was the Elijah figure for whom God's people had waited for so long. Like Elijah, John the Baptist wore a garment made of camel's hair with a leather belt (2 Kings 1.8; Mark 1.6); like Elijah, he challenged the king of his day about behaviour (1 Kings 18.17–18; Mark 6.17). In case we are left in any doubt at all, he was even explicitly identified with Elijah later on in the Gospel (Mark 9.11–13).

The new Elijah had appeared, as God promised he would. The scene is set. Anticipation rises. God promised his messenger would come and now he has. The time has come to turn the page, to roll the scroll on further, and discover what new thing God had in store for his people.

One of the striking features of this opening is that, despite Mark's description of verses 2–3 as a quotation from Isaiah, the reference is more wide ranging than this. Verse 3, as we will see in the next section, is indeed a quote from Isaiah 40.3 but verse 2 comes from Malachi 3.1 (see above) with a resonance of Exodus 23.20 ('I am going to send an angel in front of you, to guard you on the way and to bring you to the place that I have prepared') as well for good measure. It is easy to see why they fit together in Mark's mind – all of them are promises by God and all promise a secure and glorious future for his people. Putting them together states as clearly, you could that the time of waiting was over. The long-awaited moment had come. God was on the move.

We no longer wait quite as the people of God were waiting in Mark 1. Jesus' life, death and resurrection changed the world for ever but it can often feel as though we are still waiting. Lent is a time in which to remind ourselves that, now as then, God *is* on the move but that sometimes the busyness of our lives, the demands of family and friends, the stresses and strains within and without, cloud our vision. Lent is a time to make space – however we do it – a space that enables us to journey into the wide places of the wilderness so that our senses can readjust and feel once more the gentle but insistent love of God.

8

Mark 1.3–4 ... the voice of one crying out in the wilderness: 'Prepare the way of the Lord, make his paths straight,' John the baptizer appeared in the wilderness.

Isaiah 40.3–4 A voice cries out: 'In the wilderness prepare the way of the LORD, make straight in the desert a highway for our God. Every valley shall be lifted up, and every mountain and hill be made low; the uneven ground shall become level, and the rough places a plain.'

If you are alert you may have noticed that the wilderness is in a different place in Mark's quotation of Isaiah 40.3 than it is in Isaiah itself. The difference lies in what is in the wilderness. In Mark it is the voice that is in the wilderness ('the voice of one crying out in the wilderness'); in Isaiah it is the preparation that will take place in the wilderness ('In the wilderness prepare the way of the LORD'). You may feel, with entire justification, that this is an overly picky point but, in my view, it is fascinating. Isaiah 40.3 reveals what the Hebrew text says; Mark uses what the Greek translation (the Septuagint) has. The difference between the two is that if you take the Hebrew version of the verse, John the Baptist could, technically, have stayed at home in comfort and simply announced that the preparation would take place in the wilderness.

When put like that, the whole point of what is going on here becomes clear. John needed to be in the wilderness so that he could summon people there to prepare for the long-awaited arrival of the Lord. An entirely literal reading of the Hebrew might suggest otherwise, but that would be to miss the point of what was going on. John the Baptist had to be in the wilderness, no other place would have done, nor was he the only prophet to go out into the wilderness. Many others in the first century, including the Essenes, all went out into the wilderness to proclaim their message that God would return.

Although we might find this an odd move, it would have made perfect sense to a first-century Jewish audience. It is also worth pointing out that John the Baptist didn't go to any old patch of wilderness. He went to a particular and significant part of the wilderness. The wilderness around the river Jordan held an especial place in the imagination of God's people. It was the place where God's people entered the Promised Land in the first place. Isaiah's language in chapter 40 suggests that it would also be the place to which God would return to his people after the Babylonian exile. If you were going to proclaim God's return, the only place to go would be the wilderness by the river Jordan. Not going there would be like announcing the arrival of a train from the comfort of your own living room. It can be done but it is far more obvious to be at a train station awaiting the train's arrival.

Often symbols speak as powerfully, if not more powerfully, than words themselves. John's appearance in the wilderness, dressed in a manner evocative of Elijah, said all that needed to be said. Elijah had come. The messenger that went before God's face had arrived. He was to be found in the wilderness, the place where God's arrival was to be expected. The scene was set. All that was needed, now, was God's arrival as he had promised.

We who are reading Mark's text, with the benefit of hindsight and hefty hints set out before us, can now appreciate that 'the Lord' whom the messenger preceded and whose way he prepared was Jesus himself. But there is nothing in Mark to suggest that anyone other than John the Baptist recognized the significance of his arrival. It is not even easy to discern whether anyone expected an actual divine arrival in the desert close to the place where Joshua first entered the Promised Land, or whether the crowds who flocked out to John simply saw him as a symbol of something new. They clearly recognized something important was taking place but the Gospels all suggest that they were blinded by expectation. Whatever they expected, they did not see in Jesus an answer to that expectation; not then, not during his ministry, and not even as he hung dying on a cross.

It is a sobering reminder that going out into the wilderness, whatever form it takes, is no guarantee of the recognition of God. God's appearance in our midst time and time again takes an unexpected form. Following John the Baptist and Jesus into the wilderness is a good start, but no more than that.

9

Mark 1:4–6 John the baptizer appeared in the wilderness, proclaiming a baptism of repentance for the forgiveness of sins. And people from the whole Judean countryside and all the people of Jerusalem were going out to him, and were baptized by him in the river Jordan, confessing their sins. Now John was clothed with camel's hair, with a leather belt around his waist, and he ate locusts and wild honey.

Malachi 4:6 Lo, I will send you the prophet Elijah before the great and terrible day of the LORD comes. He will turn the hearts of parents to their children and the hearts of children to their parents, so that I will not come and strike the land with a curse.

In case we are left in any doubt that John was indeed a prophet like Elijah, John came proclaiming a baptism of repentance. This takes us back again to Malachi. The Elijah who was to come to prepare the way of the Lord (Malachi 3.1) was also sent to turn the hearts of the parents to their children and children to their parents. The Hebrew word for turn (*shub*) can also be translated as 'repent'. Thus in Hebrew, repentance takes place when you turn around. John the Baptist came not only looking like the long-awaited Elijah figure from Malachi, he came proclaiming the same message too.

One of the challenges we face these days is that much of the language we have always used to describe Christian faith and disposition sounds alien to people of no faith or who are new to faith. It can even sound a bit odd to those of us who have been Christians for a very long time. The world in which we live simply does not comprehend words like 'sin' and 'repentance'. They sound peculiar, condemnatory and outlandish. It isn't that people no longer mess things up. It is simply that the word 'sin' bears with it such heavy historical baggage, while at the same time not being used often in normal speech, that it is hard for it to make emotional sense to many people these days.[3] The task of translation summons us to find ways to communicate these ideas but in ways that make sense in our modern world.

The same is true of the word 'repentance'. Repentance – vital though it remains – evokes, in my mind at least, images more akin to the ancient and medieval worlds than to our own. Although probably not intentional, it can feel sometimes within the Christian tradition as though we are stuck in a permanently revolving door of repentance, so that barely have we repented of our sins than we remind ourselves of our sinfulness once more. Unless we are careful, the word 'repentance' can become a byword for the reminder that we are not good enough. It can so easily become the encouragement to wallow in our failings.

3 This issue is dealt with brilliantly by Francis Spufford in his 2012 book *Unapologetic: Why, Despite Everything, Christianity Can Still Make Surprising Emotional Sense*, Faber and Faber.

A proper theology of repentance needs to have space within it for us to live in the warm sunlight of the knowledge of our forgiveness. In the midst of this I find the image suggested by Malachi 4.6 to be powerfully affective: the turning of the hearts of parents to children and children to parents; to this we might add the turning of the hearts of humans towards one another and towards God. The point about turning our hearts to each other and to God is that, once turned, they will face each other once more. Once we have turned our hearts, we have the opportunity of deep relationship. A relationship that comes from the fact that we now face each other full on in truth and love. Of course, because we are after all human, we will turn away again and need to turn back, but this kind of language reminds us what we are turning for.

The purpose of repentance is not to remind us of how bad we are. It is not to fill us with self-loathing at our inadequacies and failings. Its purpose is to turn us to God and to one another so that we can live the life of love for which God created us.

$$\mathcal{\oslash}$$

10

Mark 1:1.1–2 and 9–11 The beginning of the good news of Jesus Christ, the Son of God. As it is written in the prophet Isaiah, 'See, I am sending my messenger ahead of you, who will prepare your way … In those days Jesus came from Nazareth of Galilee and was baptized by John in the Jordan. And just as he was coming up out of the water, he saw the heavens torn apart and the Spirit descending like a dove on him. And a voice came from heaven, 'You are my Son, the Beloved; with you I am well pleased.'

Malachi 3.1 *See, I am sending my messenger to prepare the way before me*

One of the glories of reading (or listening) to a story is that we provide the backdrop, the scenery and the extras. Our imaginations are invited to join in the glorious task of story telling, providing the key details that bring the narrative to life. This is why it is often hard to see a film based on one of your favourite books – it just looks wrong. The Gospels are no different. Just as much as with any piece of English litera-ture, the Gospels invite our imaginations to the story and invite us to stretch out the backdrop, paint the scenery, and provide not only the extras but the key proponents too. As we have already noted, this whole story takes place against the ambiguous backdrop of the terrifying, life-bringing wilderness. What we need to do now is to populate the scene. There is John the Baptist, of course, the crowd from Jerusalem and Jesus, but Mark's suggests that there is another character as well looking on.

One of the striking features of Mark's use of the Malachi quote is that the pronoun is different. In Malachi God declares that he is sending 'my' messenger to prepare the way before 'me'; in Mark the quote declares that 'my' messenger is sent ahead of 'you'. In other words, the audience of God's statement has changed. In Malachi God addressed his people who were awaiting salvation; in Mark he ad-dressed someone else – not the people who are about to be saved but the one who will be doing the saving.

The best answer to the question of who God might be talking to in this verse is, of course, Jesus. John the Baptist did prepare Jesus' way and God addressed Jesus again as 'you' a few verses later at his baptism ('You are my Son, the Beloved; with you I am well pleased', Mark 1.11). This all gives this passage a different eye view than we often have in mind. We are human and so our eye view is, naturally, that of the human world. We see events from our perspective – why would we not? – but here Mark invites us to approach his narrative with an additional lens in mind. Of course we are interested in John's message and in the people who flock out to hear him, but Mark reminds us that there is another dimension altogether to this most important story. It is a dimension that we can all too easily miss unless we remain alert.

The story that is about to unfold is God's story and right at the start God sets it in motion. This opening scene occurs exactly in the place that you would expect God to return – the wilderness. It involves a character long promised by God – an Elijah figure sent to prepare the way. It involves a character commissioned by God – Jesus sent to save God's people. And yet with a human eye view nothing out of the ordinary was observable. All you could see was an eccentrically clothed prophet calling for repentance. Mark even hints that it was only Jesus who heard God's voice after his baptism – no one else noticed anything out of the ordinary.

This is a narrative, then, that we are invited to view at two levels – the human and the divine. Seeing it like this reminds us that this is not the only narrative that we are invited to observe in this way. Our own world and the lives that we live can also be viewed solely from a human perspective or from God's eye view too. Just like the people of Jesus' day, we often cannot see what God can see, but with care, and if we are alert to those things of God, we might just catch a glimpse of a different way of viewing the world and remember that what we can see is not all that there is.

11

Mark 1:12 And the Spirit immediately drove him out into the wilderness.

The very first thing that the Spirit did after it descended on Jesus was to drive him into the wilderness. You may be forgiven for being a little confused at this point. Surely he was already in the wilderness? John the Baptist had gone into the wilderness to announce the preparation of the way of the Lord; Jesus had met him there and been baptized. How is it, then, that the Spirit can drive him into the wilderness?

One option for understanding this detail is that Mark does, occasionally, appear to get his locations confused so that Jesus is reported as crossing the Sea of Galilee only to end up on the same side as he began (see Mark 8.10 and 22). It is possible that the same thing is happening here and Mark has forgotten that Jesus was already in the wilderness.

More likely, however, is that Mark is trying to communicate something greater than a purely physical location, as indeed is often the case with his other geographical bloopers. In Mark the language of crossing to the other side signals that a moment of transformation is around the corner; in the same way going out into the wilderness suggests that redemption is on its way. This theme is so important within the Gospel that Mark could be reminding us of its importance here; it is also possible, however, that this repeated theme of wilderness is nothing more than that, a repeated motif. I shall leave it up to you to decide.

If the wilderness theme *is* important then this use of it stands as a reminder of yet another strand that was often attached to the wilderness in the Bible – that of the wilderness being the place where people could hear God's call. Moses heard it at the burning bush in Exodus 3.1–9; Elijah heard it in the cave at Mount Horeb after fleeing through the wilderness in 1 Kings 19.1–13; even Paul reports that after his conversion he went out to Arabia (Galatians 1.17). The wilderness was seen as a place of danger and redemption but it was also, as it remains today, a place of solitude and spaciousness. Life can so often be a maelstrom of pressure and activity. It can provide such competing constraints that, unless we are adept at listening for it, there is little hope of hearing the voice of God above the clamour of everyday living.[4]

Of course, Mark doesn't tell us precisely why the Spirit drove Jesus off into the wilderness. In his case it wasn't to hear God's voice in the first place, since God had already spoken in both verses 2 and 11. Nor is there any hint that Jesus, unlike many Old Testament characters such as Moses (Exodus 3.11—4.13) or Jonah (Jonah 1.3), was attempting to get out of his calling by running away. He was tempted by Satan (as the next verse tells us) but the suggestion hangs in the air that the wilderness provided more than temptation – it provided space for assimilation, for reflection and for preparation. Time in the wilderness may well have provided Jesus with his last few moments of focused spaciousness before his ministry began – a ministry that was often marked by Jesus' attempt to withdraw from the crowds only to be followed by them.

Lent is a time that challenges us to reflect on our own need of focused spaciousness. A space that can allow us time for assimilation, reflection, preparation, and sometimes hearing God speak at all. A very few people might be able actually to withdraw into a wild place for the forty days of Lent, but the vast majority of us would have neither the time nor the desire for this. The question is what we *can* do to find this space. The answer will be different for each one of us at each specific moment in our lives, but it is a question very much worth asking.

---

4 It is possible to become adept at listening to God's voice in the clamour of the everyday (for more on this see, my previous book *Everyday God: The Spirit of the Ordinary*, SCM Press, 2014) but it can be hard to do.

12

Mark 1.13 He was in the wilderness for forty days, tempted by Satan; and he was with the wild beasts; and the angels waited on him.

We have, at last, reached Mark's temptation narrative or, more accurately, his temptation sentence. Somewhat tantalizingly in this short but meaty sentence three groups of characters are introduced: Satan, the wild beasts and the angels. These three are a somewhat motley crew and, at first glance, it is not too easy to see what connection they might have with one another, apart from the fact that they were all with Jesus in the wilderness.

In reality, however, as with so much else, Mark was making a profound theological point in this small but significant sentence. A few bits of background will help to illuminate what kind of a point it was. Lurking in the background of this story is the story of another temptation narrative – a narrative that made this narrative necessary in the first place – the story of the temptation of Eve and Adam in the Garden of Eden. It is, of course, common to see the serpent in the Garden as Satan; less well-known is the post-biblical tradition that Adam and Eve were fed by ministering angels in the Garden of Eden, so that they didn't have to work the land in order to eat.[5] Between these two in Mark 1.13 are the wild beasts who, like those in Eden and like those in the prophecies of God's promised future (e.g. Isaiah 11.6–9 where the lion lies down with the lamb), appear to coexist in harmony with each other and with Jesus.

In other words, Mark's simple, startlingly short sentence makes a statement that is loud and clear. The old, old story

---

5 See, for example, Babylonian Sanhedrin 59b which contains: 'Adam reclined in the Garden of Eden, whilst the ministering angels roasted flesh and strained wine for him'.

has begun again. At the dawn of time, in the harmony and peace of the Garden of Eden, Eve and Adam were tempted and fell. The new Adam, Jesus, was, like them, ministered to by angels and was, like them, tempted by Satan, this time not in a garden but in the wilderness, a place poised between danger and redemption, but he resisted. And in his resistance he ushered in a new dawn in which the wild animals lived in harmony together and in which God came to save his people.

Mark has, thus far in his narrative, taken his readers gently by the hand, showing them sign after sign of hope and redemption. In this verse it is almost as though he took out a trumpet and blew it in our ears as loudly as he could. The backdrop of the narrative is the wilderness, the place Isaiah declared to be where people should prepare for God's return; Jesus' coming had been announced by an Elijah-type figure as Malachi had stated it would be; his identity and calling were proclaimed by God from heaven and then Jesus, the new Adam, was tempted by Satan, ministered to by angels and lived peacefully with wild animals. There is little more that Mark could have done to indicate that the long-awaited moment had come and that the world was about to change for ever.

The very next sentence in Mark, however ('Now after John was arrested, Jesus came to Galilee, proclaiming the good news of God', Mark 1.14), moves from the wilderness to Galilee; from a wide space to everyday life; from the ringing clarity of the announcement of redemption to the hurly burly of ministry. Almost at once the clarity faded. The disciples, who jumped up to follow Jesus when he called, went on to display little comprehension of who he really was. The crowd was amazed again and again, but their amazement led them nowhere. The scribes, Pharisees and Chief Priests were downright hostile.

It is, perhaps, reassuring to those of us who wrestle day

in and day out to follow Jesus and to proclaim the Kingdom that, even following a start as good as the one we see in Mark 1.1–13, people still did not work out who Jesus was and why he had come. Of course Mark's account is written with hindsight, and hindsight always provides us with a much clearer vision of God and his purposes, but nevertheless it is worth reminding ourselves that Jesus was still Jesus even when few people noticed who he was and the world still changed even when no one recognized what was going on. The reality of God's action has never been dependent on human recognition, no matter what form it took.

Mark's account of Jesus' 'temptation' introduces powerful themes: themes of hope and redemption; of identity and recognition. Probably more than any other Gospel writer Mark reminds us of the ambiguity of the wilderness as a place balanced between terror and clarity; despair and hope; death and renewal. Difficult though it be, the wilderness offers us a gift, and the beginning of Mark's Gospel is one of the places where the nature of that gift is probed, explored and unpacked.

At the start of Lent, we are prompted to reflect on our own experiences of wilderness in all their ambiguity – those that uplift us and those that crush us; those that bring hope and those that oppress us with despair; those in which we hear God's voice calling clearly and those in which it feels as though God is, and will always be, absent. It also challenges us to reflect on whether, like the people of Jesus' day, the signs of God's presence are all around us in letters six feet tall but, for a whole host of reasons, we are unable to see them for what they are.

Questions for discussion and reflection

Reflecting on Scripture

- Read Mark 1.2–13 out loud, slowly.
- Spend a minute or two in silence reflecting on what you heard.
- Read it again, this time listen out for words and phrases that jump out at you as important.
- Spend some time sharing the words and phrases that jumped out as you heard it read, and reflect together on why they were so important for you this time.

Discuss

Recognizing the signs

In his account, Mark takes care and effort to establish the importance of the events taking place:

- Why do you think it was so important to Mark's story to make clear that his story began where the Old Testament left off?
- In the light of your reflections on the wilderness last time, what importance would *you* attach to John going out to the wilderness to proclaim his message?
- Despite the heavy hints dropped about the significance of John the Baptist, it seems that most people completely missed the significance of what was going on. Why do you think they (and we) find it so hard to recognize the presence and action of God?

Repentance

The heart of both John the Baptist and Jesus' message was repentance:

- What does the word 'repentance' mean to you? Do you find it a helpful or unhelpful word?
- Why do you think that, today, many people struggle with the concept of repentance?
- If you were to use another word instead of 'repent', which one would you choose?
- What is lost if, whatever word we use, we avoid the idea of repentance?

Hearing God's voice

One of the themes we observed was that, for some people, God's voice was heard more clearly in the desert.

- Some people find silence essential to hearing God's voice; others find it stultifying and oppressive. Where do you hear God speaking to you most clearly?
- If you were to go somewhere in the hope of hearing God speak, where would you go?

A garden and a desert

- What difference does it make to Mark's account of Jesus in the wilderness to think of it as a reversal of Adam and Eve in the Garden of Eden?

3

WHO ARE YOU?

Jesus and the Devil in Matthew

Matthew's account of Jesus' temptation – like its companion in Luke's Gospel – is much fuller and more extensive than Mark's. In both Matthew and Luke, Jesus spent forty days and forty nights in the wilderness before being tempted. In both, the devil challenged Jesus in the same three ways: to turn stone(s) into bread;[6] to throw himself from the pinnacle of the temple; and to fall down and worship the devil. In both, two out of the three questions begin with the phrase 'If you are the Son of God…' In both, the temptations begin in the wilderness but do not remain there as Jesus is taken by the devil to a high mountain (in Matthew, though in Luke he is simply led 'up') and to the temple in Jerusalem.

The question that emerges as we read these longer temptation narratives is what was really going on? What was Jesus being tempted to be or do? And what can we learn in our own Christian discipleship from how Jesus responded to the devil's challenges? It is this question that forms the heart of this next chapter.

The reflections in this passage will all focus on Matthew 4.1–10; again you may like to read the whole of that passage before you read on.

Matthew 4.1–10 Then Jesus was led up by the Spirit into the wilderness to be tempted by the devil. He fasted for forty

6 In Matthew it is stones in the plural; in Luke a single stone.

days and forty nights, and afterwards he was famished. The tempter came and said to him, 'If you are the Son of God, command these stones to become loaves of bread.' But he answered, 'It is written, "One does not live by bread alone, but by every word that comes from the mouth of God."' Then the devil took him to the holy city and placed him on the pinnacle of the temple, saying to him, 'If you are the Son of God, throw yourself down; for it is written, "He will command his angels concerning you," and "On their hands they will bear you up, so that you will not dash your foot against a stone."' Jesus said to him, 'Again it is written, "Do not put the Lord your God to the test."' Again, the devil took him to a very high mountain and showed him all the kingdoms of the world and their splendor; and he said to him, 'All these I will give you, if you will fall down and worship me.' Jesus said to him, 'Away with you, Satan! for it is written, "Worship the Lord your God, and serve only him."'

13

Matthew 4.1 *Then Jesus was led up by the Spirit into the wilderness to be tempted by the devil.*

What comes to mind when you hear the word 'temptation'? The word is a powerful one. It drips seductiveness, suggesting that resistance will be a struggle. It intimates that the siren call of that for which we yearn will summon us, time and time again, so that we may well crumble and give in to its call. The advertising industry is wise to the power of temptation and many adverts are based on the assumption that, if whatever is being offered is made tempting enough, we will simply not be able to resist it.

For some, Lent is all about resisting temptation, so that the point of giving something up is in order to hone skills in the resistance of temptation that we may well need when a greater and more powerful temptation crosses our path. There is no doubt that these are vital lessons to learn. In today's world it is, perhaps, even more vital than it has ever been to be people who learn to be content with who we are and what we have; people who are not swayed by the vast numbers of passing temptations that cross our paths.

The question is whether the account of Jesus' own 'temptations' gives us the model for this. Indeed it is fascinating that the words 'tempt' and 'temptation' are so thoroughly associated with the exchange between Jesus and the devil. In English, 'tempt' and 'temptation' imply that something attractive is on offer, so attractive in fact that it lures you inexorably into action. Often, but not always, this 'something' is sinful and seductive in its sinfulness. The question is whether this was what was going on between Jesus and the devil. Certainly the thought of bread, after forty days and nights of fasting, must have been very attractive. The NRSV chooses the somewhat quaint word 'famished' to describe Jesus' hunger, but was the challenge to cast himself from the top of a temple or to bow down to worship the devil equally attractive?

The word translated as 'tempt' is the Greek word *peirazō* which, when used elsewhere in Matthew, is translated as 'test'. So in Matthew 16.1 the Pharisees and Sadducees tested Jesus by asking him for a sign from heaven; or in 19.3 the Pharisees asked for his view on divorce. In both cases Jesus' questioners would dearly have loved to trip him up but there is little implication that he was being tempted to sin. Rather, what they were doing was challenging and testing Jesus to discern how he would respond under pressure. In this sense this was also what the devil was doing here. It is also worth noticing that Jesus was in the wilderness in the first place at the behest of the Spirit; in other words, his encounter with the devil was within the plan of God. Jesus and the devil did not sneak away for a bit of illicit tempting; the Spirit led him there.

All of this suggests that it might be better to translate what went on between Jesus and the devil as 'testing' rather than 'tempting'. As we saw in the introduction, this makes particular sense of the formulation the devil used in his first two questions to Jesus: 'If you are the Son of God ...' By this point in Matthew's Gospel there is no doubt that Matthew thought that Jesus was the Son of God. There is little in the text to imply that the devil doubted it either. The question, therefore, is not so much about *whether* Jesus was the Son of God as *what kind* of Son of God he would be.

The devil was testing Jesus to see if he would take the hard route or the easy one. Would he be the kind of Son of God who would use his miracles to his own advantage – to feed himself when hungry – or for the good of others? Would he be the kind of Son of God that took drastic actions – like throwing himself off the temple – to force God into action against his plan? Would he be the kind of Son of God that would do anything at all – like bowing down to the devil – in order to gain power in this world? The devil was asking provocative questions and laying down challenges that would reveal the choices that Jesus would make about what kind of Son of God he would be.

If we are to follow Jesus' own example in Lent, it might be helpful to think about testing as much as about tempta-tion. For us the question is what kind of disciple are we? What will we do and who will we be? If we can arrive at the end of Lent with a clear answer to this question – as clear as Jesus' to the devil – then our Lent will have been well spent.

14

Matthew 4.1–3, 10 *Then Jesus was led up by the Spirit into the wilderness to be tempted by the devil. He fasted for forty days and forty nights, and afterwards he was famished. The tempter came and said to him, 'If you are the Son of God, command these stones to become loaves of bread' … Jesus said to him, 'Away with you, Satan!'*

In the Bible, the role of satan isn't always entirely evil.

Before you throw up your hands in horror, let me explain what I mean. The word *satan* in Hebrew means 'accuser'. In the book of Job he is called 'the satan' – it's a job title rather than a name. Only later in books like 1 Chronicles (21.2) and Zechariah (3.1–2) does it become a name – 'Satan' – rather than a role – 'the satan'.

Nevertheless, in all of these examples the accuser's role was to ask questions. In the book of Job he suggested that if Job were to be cursed then he would be less devout than he was when blessed. God gave him permission to test his theory. The book of Job is the answer. In Zechariah Satan stood ready to accuse the new High Priest, Joshua, but in this case God rebuked him and would not allow him to accuse him.

The devil we meet in Matthew 4 is quite like this. He accuses Jesus, in the sense of challenging him and testing to see what his response will be. Indeed it is interesting that Matthew gives him three different names – the devil (4.1); the tempter or tester (4.3); and Satan (4.10). This highlights that, even here in Matthew, his job is asking questions, probing and challenging, to find a response.

This is the last occasion in the sweep of the biblical narrative when the devil's task is as much probing and questioning, as it is outright rebellion and opposition. As we go through the Bible, the devil's role becomes more and more consistently evil, as he opposes God time after time to the extent that in the end all he does is oppose God. It is probably also worth noting that this is not the only place where the devil has a range of titles. Later on in Matthew itself, other names are used, like 'Beelzebub' (12.24),[7] 'evil one' (13.38) and 'enemy' (13.39). This variety is even greater elsewhere in the Bible (see, for example, Lucifer, Isaiah 14.12, or Belial, 2 Corinthians 6.15).

The devil, then, has a range of titles and even a range of roles. None of them are good but not all are equally evil. In some places in Scripture the evil the devil represents, the catastrophe that comes in his wake, the life-destroying effects of demons in people's lives, and the consequences of rebellion against God are all too clear. In others, as here, his opposition is limited to asking testing questions.

There is a vital role of testing, probing and challenging which gets to the heart of who people really are and the choices they will make. The skill of sifting the challenge, of discerning the true nature of vocation and of remaining true to our calling is a vital one for Christian life and faith. What Jesus reveals in this story is the ability to stay true to who we are in the face of testing and temptation. Here Jesus shows us how it's done.

It is striking that Jesus allowed the devil to ask his three questions before dismissing him ('Away with you, Satan', 4.10). In other words, although he could – and later did – tell the devil to depart, he permitted the testing to take place. If he had not responded to the devil's testing as he did the results would have been disastrous, but he *did* stand firm – and in doing so revealed a rich pattern of behaviour for us to follow in such situations. It is not testing itself that is the problem, so much as, in the face of testing, losing sight of who we are called to be.

---

7 Scholars are not entirely clear where this name comes from. In the Old Testament there is a reference to Ba'al Zebub, or Baal of the flies. In other Jewish texts Beelzebul is the Prince of demons.

15

Matthew 4.2–4 He fasted for forty days and forty nights, and afterwards he was famished. The tempter came and said to him, 'If you are the Son of God, command these stones to become loaves of bread.' But he answered, 'It is written, "One does not live by bread alone, but by every word that comes from the mouth of God."'

Every culture around the world has set-piece scenes that communicate far more than the words or actions alone. In Western society, if we see someone down on one knee and holding a ring, then we will have clear expectations about what this action means and what that person is about to say. In the same way, within the Bible certain scenes communicate far more than the words they use. We have already noticed the importance of the wilderness and the complex mix of expectations that the word evokes. Another example is a man and woman meeting at a well: a scene that sets up expectations that a marriage will soon follow (expectations that lurk powerfully behind the exchange between Jesus and the Samaritan woman in John 4).

The scene here is similarly evocative. The fact that Jesus was in the wilderness for forty days and forty nights and then quoted three verses from Deuteronomy 6—8 (8.5 in verse 4; 6.16 in verse 7, and 6.13 in verse 10) evokes the wilderness wanderings of God's people after the Exodus and before they settled in the Promised Land. Jesus was in the wilderness for forty days and nights; God's people were in the wilderness for forty years. Deuteronomy 8.5–20 makes clear that the wandering in the wilderness was meant to teach God's people the very important lesson of faithfulness to and trust in God. During their time in the wilderness,

God's people needed to learn three key lessons: that they could not live by bread alone (8.5); that they should not test and question God (6.16), and that they should only worship God and no one else (6.13). Even the briefest of readings of the stories indicates that, to put it mildly, God's people did not learn these lessons easily. Time and time again they faltered and failed.

If you add into the picture the fact that God identified his people as his first born son ('thus says the LORD: Israel is my firstborn son', Exodus 4.22), then it becomes easier to see the significance of this whole scene (and the reason why Jesus had to allow the devil to test him three times *before* dismissing him). The Son of God has returned to the wilderness once more. For forty days and nights he has wandered with no food or drink but, unlike his forebears, he did not falter and fail.

He was tested just as they were but responded quite differently: his faithfulness never waivered. In Deuteronomy the verses quoted flow outwards from that most important of verses: 'You shall love the LORD your God with all your heart, and with all your soul, and with all your might' (Deuteronomy 6.5). In the wilderness, Jesus lived his love of God with heart, soul and might. In the wilderness, he showed us the way to be true children of God. In the wilderness, he broke the cycle of failure and faltering that had hitherto so marked the keeping of the covenant.

All of this begins to make clear that this most iconic of passages is as much about us as it is about Jesus. The story has begun again. Earlier in Matthew's Gospel in the birth narratives, Jesus was called out of Egypt, just as his ancestors had been ('Out of Egypt I have called my son', Matthew 2.15). He wandered in the wilderness, just like them. He was tested, just as they had been. But there the similarity ended. God's Son had gone out into the wilderness, where redemption was expected to begin, and modelled such profound faithfulness that God's story of redemptive love could begin again.

Jesus' testing in the wilderness changed everything. He broke the pattern of wilderness wandering and opened the door into a new way of being, a way of being in which we, walking in the footsteps of the one who summons us to follow him, can express our love of God with the whole of our being, heart, soul and might.

16

Matthew 4.4 *But he answered, 'It is written, "One does not live by bread alone, but by every word that comes from the mouth of God."'*

Deuteronomy 8.3 *He humbled you by letting you hunger, then by feeding you with manna, with which neither you nor your ancestors were acquainted, in order to make you understand that one does not live by bread alone, but by every word that comes from the mouth of the LORD.*

We have a tendency to become so fixed on what we want that we fail to notice what we need. There is something about human nature that focuses so much on our immediate needs that, once they are fulfilled, we believe ourselves to be satisfied. Not only that but the minute our immediate problem is solved we try to go it alone, independent of the help upon which only a moment ago we depended.

The story of the feeding of God's people with manna in Exodus 16, to which Deuteronomy 8.3 refers, is an excellent example of who we are and who we are called to be. It is very striking in Exodus to notice that only one chapter after Moses had led the people across the miraculously parted Red Sea, they started to grumble and wished they were back in slavery in Egypt because they were hungry. As we noticed in chapter 1, God's people might have been free in their bodies, but their minds were still in slavery.

God listened to their complaints and gave them quails to eat in the evening and a bread-like substance in the morning, which they called 'what is it?' (in Hebrew, *manna*). God told them not to keep the *manna* overnight as new *manna* would be given every day but, of course, some did keep it, in an attempt to help themselves so that they would not have to rely entirely on God.

Deuteronomy 8.3 is a reflection on the whole episode and observes that it was designed to teach the people to rely on God for everything in their lives. The key to understanding the verse is the word 'live'. It is tempting to respond to the statement that 'one does not live by bread alone' with the age-old pantomime response – 'oh yes you can'. The point is that someone might just be able to survive by bread alone (so long as water was available as well). They might not be very well on such a diet but they could survive; they might 'be alive' but they would not truly live.

The provision of bread might assuage an immediate gnawing hunger but limping from meal to meal is survival, not living. A focus solely on bread (or its modern equivalent) also encourages us to focus solely on our own desires and concerns, rather than those of people around us. It pulls our gaze inwards to ourselves and downwards to what concerns us now at this very moment.

In contrast, real living lifts our gaze outwards and upwards. Real living involves relying on all the words that come from the mouth of God. God is not just the God who sends *manna* at mealtimes. The words that came from the mouth of God were what brought the world into being in the first place. The words of God sustain creation. The words of God bring comfort, healing and hope. The words of God cry out for justice and peace. The list goes on and on. The words of

God summon us beyond our own immediate needs and concerns. They remind us that God created the whole world, not just us. They call us to join in with caring for that world. They send us with that message of comfort, healing and hope to all those we meet. They demand that we struggle with every fibre of our being for God's Kingdom to be present on earth as in heaven.

Jesus, of course, knew all of this. This is why, not only here but throughout his ministry, he refused to reduce what was going on to his own needs and concerns. We should be clear that this is not a calling to an unhealthy ignoring of our own needs to the extent that we burn out and become exhausted. It is simply a vocation to avoid focusing on ourselves, and what we want, to the exclusion of all else. The challenge we face is to reflect on what it means not to live by bread alone today. Where in our lives do we drag our vision inwards and downwards, rather than outwards and upwards? How can we learn to rely more fully and whole-heartedly on every word that comes from the mouth of God?

17

Matthew 4.5–7 *Then the devil took him to the holy city and placed him on the pinnacle of the temple, saying to him, 'If you are the Son of God, throw yourself down; for it is written, "He will command his angels concerning you", and "On their hands they will bear you up, so that you will not dash your foot against a stone."' Jesus said to him, 'Again it is written, "Do not put the Lord your God to the test."'*

Psalm 91.11–12 *For he will command his angels concerning you to guard you in all your ways. On their hands they will bear you up, so that you will not dash your foot against a stone.*

Deuteronomy 6.16 *Do not put the* LORD *your God to the test, as you tested him at Massah.*

You do not have to spend very long in a Christian context before you encounter 'proof-text Ping-Pong': I serve a verse at you, and you block and send one back to me. It is a popular past time in many parts of our churches and is never a good idea. At first glance, you might imagine that both the devil and Jesus were engaged in a grand game of proof-text Ping-Pong here. The devil lobbed a verse at Jesus and Jesus blocked and countered him with another verse.

Although initially they may appear to have been using Scripture in the same way – picking verses out of context to prove a point – in practice what they were doing was very different indeed. The heart of the difference lies in what each of the verses meant in their original context.

The verse the devil quoted comes from Psalm 91, which talks about the life-long faithfulness of the God who is our shelter (v. 1). In this Psalm the Psalmist talks eloquently about God being our refuge and fortress (v. 2); covering us with his wings [pinions] like a hawk does their food (v. 4); and providing us with safety and security. The verses quoted by the devil here are in this context of the knowledge of God's constant care for us. The key point of the Psalm comes towards the end of it in verse 15: 'When they call to me, I will answer them; I will be with them in trouble, I will rescue them and honour them'. In other words, God stands ready to help whenever we need it. What the devil was inviting Jesus to do was to simulate need – to place himself in great and unnecessary danger in order to test whether the God who offered help in trouble would really help. He was challenging Jesus to put his life in danger voluntarily.

Jesus in great contrast used his verse in precisely the right way. The story referred to in Deuteronomy 6.16 again refers back to Exodus; this time to chapter 17. Shortly after God had fed the people with quails and manna, they began to complain again. This time their complaint was about being thirsty. More importantly, though, they began grumbling that they didn't know whether God was with them or not. Indeed Moses became so frightened by their complaints that he feared they were going to stone him. God provided yet again – telling Moses to strike the rock in order to produce water. The people had learnt half a good lesson but not the other half. They had learnt that God could and would provide for them but went about asking for it in entirely the wrong way: doubting the very presence of God when God didn't do exactly what they wanted.[8]

Jesus' response reveals that he was aware that what the devil was inviting him to do was exactly what the Israelites did at Massah – not to trust that God is who he says he is and to force him to act according to their own agenda. Even the devil's use of Scripture – using it for his own ends rather than seeking to understand what it is about – reveals a similar attitude. Tempting though it be, we need to resist mimicking this kind of behaviour. Prayer is notoriously tricky to get right – God loves us and likes us to ask for what we really need but how easy it is for this to tip into testing him, trying to force him to act according to our agenda, not his. The key lies in trust that God really is who he says he is and that he knows what is best for the world and we don't.

18

Matthew 4.8–11 Again, the devil took him to a very high mountain and showed him all the kingdoms of the world and their splendour; and he said to him, 'All these I will

8 The word *Massah* in Hebrew means 'test', so its name serves as a reminder about their actions there.

give you, if you will fall down and worship me.' Jesus said
to him, 'Away with you, Satan! for it is written, "Worship
the Lord your God, and serve only him."' Then the devil left
him, and suddenly angels came and waited on him.

Deuteronomy 6.13 *The Lord your God you shall fear; him*
you shall serve, and by his name alone you shall swear.

For the devil's third test the location changed again. Between
the first and second tests, Jesus was taken from the wilderness to the temple, now he is taken to a high mountain from
which he could see all the kingdoms of the world. There is,
of course, no such mountain from which it is possible to see
all the kingdoms of the world but the image is, nevertheless,
evocative since on the top of a high mountain it can feel as
if you really can see for ever as the surrounding ground
stretches away to the horizon.

It is striking that this is the only question the devil asked
that is not prefaced by 'if you are the Son of God …' but it
is not hard to work out why that phrase was dropped. The
other two tests could, arguably, have been accepted by a Son
of God – even if it would have meant that he would have
been a self-serving, God-testing Son of God. But this test,
and in Matthew's Gospel the final test, would actually require
Jesus to change allegiance and to give up being 'Son of God'.
It would not be possible to claim any kind of relationship
with God after worshipping anyone else, let alone the devil.
This was the key moment when Jesus was asked to declare
who he really was.

One can't help asking whether the devil really had the
ability to offer Jesus 'the kingdoms of the world and their
splendour' – surely they didn't belong to him? This is the
place in these testings where we see that the devil is more
than just 'the satan' that he has been up to this point. Until
now all he has done is ask questions and lay down challenges

but here we see that he does have some level of authority over the world (because otherwise he wouldn't be able to offer it to Jesus). At various points in the New Testament, the devil is said to be the ruler of this world (see, for example, John 12.31; 14.30; 16.11; Ephesians 6.11–12). This is probably what is being alluded to here. The devil's authority – if you can call it that – is an authority limited to this world and this age and this is what he offered to Jesus here.

The irony is that at the end of the Gospel Jesus stood on another mountain in Galilee and proclaimed that 'All authority in heaven and on earth' had been given to him (Matthew 28.18). Suffering and death, in obedience to the God who loved him, gave him far more authority (in heaven as well as on earth) than that being offered to him here. Here the devil simply offered a temporary authority over this world and this age; there he received a permanent authority over heaven and earth for ever. Here the authority was offered on the basis of breaking allegiance to God and worshipping the devil instead; in Matthew 28 he received authority precisely because he had been faithful and obedient to the task that God had set before him, no matter what the cost.

In his response to this question, Jesus – at last – dismissed the devil, but he didn't dismiss the devil because he knew there was a better option around the corner. He dismissed the devil because the worship and service of God was at the core of who he was. It is incidentally worth noting that Matthew has changed the word in Deuteronomy 6.13 from 'fear' to 'worship'. In effect the two are the same. In the Old Testament 'the fear of God' (which Proverbs tells us is the beginning of wisdom) involved feelings of awe and wonder in the presence of the almighty God who created the world. Such feelings of awe lead into worship. The implication of the devil's question here is that a little worship or devotion offered in a different direction does no harm to anyone. Jesus knew that it would do great harm and, in fact, it would change the very nature of who he was. Like Jesus, we are called to recognize what can be worshipped and what should not be; such recognition is what shaped who Jesus was and what will shape who we are.

Jesus' testing by the devil in Matthew focuses strongly on the question of identity. What kind of Son of God would Jesus choose to be? As we read on in Matthew it becomes increasingly clear that the decisions that Jesus made in the company of the devil were decisions that continued to shape the whole of his ministry: a ministry shaped by a refusal to put his own desires above the needs of others, by a strong recognition of the nature of God with no need to test whether he was who he said he was, and by placing worship and service of God at the centre of everything that he did.

In its turn it challenges us to reflect for ourselves on what kind of disciples of this Son of God we will choose to be and, having made the choice, to live this choice with passion and commitment in everything that we do.

Questions for discussion and reflection

Reflecting on Scripture

- Read out Matthew 4.1–10.
- Spend a minute or two in silence reflecting on what you heard.
- Then read it again but pause after verses 4, 7 and 11.
  - After verse 4, read Deuteronomy 8.3
  - After verse 7, read Deuteronomy 6.16 and Psalm 91.11–12
  - After verse 11, read Deuteronomy 6.13
- Then discuss what hearing the passage alongside the Old Testament passages did. Did you hear anything different the second time?

Discuss

Temptation

- Talk about the words 'temptation' and 'testing'. Which one do you prefer to use when thinking about the conversation between Jesus and the devil in Matthew? Are there others we could use as well as these?
- Think about what you are doing for Lent – is resisting temptation important? If it is, discuss why it is; if not, why not.
- If, during Lent, you set yourself the challenge of testing what kind of disciple of Jesus you chose to be…what kind of things might you do to test this?

The devil

Some people don't talk about the devil at all; others talk about him a lot.

- What do you think about 'the devil'? Do you see 'him' as an actual person? The personification of the evil in our world? Or would you rather not talk about 'the devil' at all?

- What is helpful and unhelpful about the way people often talk about the devil?

- What do you think about the accuser role? When does asking questions tip into active rebellion against God?

The wilderness wanderings

- If we see Jesus' time in the wilderness as a re-living and transforming of the wilderness wanderings after the Exodus, what difference, if any, does it make?

- What do you think it means 'not to live by bread alone but by every word that comes from the mouth of God'? What would your life look like if you did this?

- You might like to talk about 'proof-texting'. When does quoting from the Bible become proof-texting? Is proof-texting always wrong?

- Who or what are people tempted to worship today that is not God?

4

TESTINGS
Jesus and Testing in Luke

As we noticed in the previous chapter, there are very strong similarities between Matthew and Luke's accounts of Jesus' testing by the devil, so you will be relieved to know that we won't go back over the same material again; much as I love a close reading of the text, there are limits to this!

This chapter is, instead, dedicated to reflecting on what is different in Luke's account of Jesus' encounter with the devil, and there are two particular differences that jump out. The first is that the last two questions are reversed in Luke, so that Jesus is first invited to worship the devil and then to jump off the temple. The second difference is that the devil was not dismissed utterly as in Matthew and merely departs until an opportune time. These two apparently small details shed a fascinating light on Luke's telling of the story of Jesus' life and ministry, and in their turn provide much food for reflection for our own journey of discipleship.

As in the previous chapters you might find it helpful to read the whole passage before we explore it in more detail.

Luke 4.1–13 Jesus, full of the Holy Spirit, returned from the Jordan and was led by the Spirit in the wilderness, where for forty days he was tempted by the devil. He ate nothing at all during those days, and when they were over, he was famished. The devil said to him, 'If you are the Son of God, command this stone to become a loaf of bread.' Jesus answered him, 'It is written, "One does not live by bread alone."' Then the devil led him up and showed him in an instant all the kingdoms of the world. And the devil said to him, 'To you I will give their glory and all this authority; for it has been given over to me, and I give it to anyone I please. If you, then, will worship me, it will all be yours.' Jesus answered him, 'It is written, "Worship the Lord your God, and serve only him."' Then the devil took him to Jerusalem, and placed him on the pinnacle of the temple, saying to him, 'If you are the Son of God, throw yourself down from here, for it is written, "He will command his angels concerning you, to protect you," and "On their hands they will bear you up, so that you will not dash your foot against a stone."' Jesus answered him, 'It is said, "Do not put the Lord your God to the test."' When the devil had finished every test, he departed from him until an opportune time.

19

Luke 4.5 –13 Then the devil led him up and showed him in an instant all the kingdoms of the world. And the devil said to him, 'To you I will give their glory and all this authority; for it has been given over to me, and I give it to anyone I please. If you, then, will worship me, it will all be yours.' Jesus answered him, 'It is written, "Worship the Lord your God, and serve only him."' Then the devil took him to Jerusalem, and placed him on the pinnacle of the temple, saying to him, 'If you are the Son of God, throw yourself down from here, for it is written, "He will command his angels concerning you, to protect you," and "On their hands they will bear you up, so that you will not dash your foot against a stone."' Jesus answered him, 'It is said, "Do not

put the Lord your God to the test."' When the devil had
finished every test, he departed from him until an opportune
time.

Unlike Matthew, Luke provides us with an answer to the
question of why the devil felt able to offer Jesus all the
kingdoms of the earth – because they have been given over
to him. In the context of Luke this is a sharp-edged jab at
the Roman Empire. In Luke 2.1, the Romans had been
identified as the keepers of the whole of the world in so
much as the Emperor Augustus demanded that 'all the world
be registered'. Luke's subtle – or not so subtle – point here
is that the glory and authority of the whole world had 'been
given over' to the devil; in other words, the current keepers
of the world – the Romans – had, knowingly or not, handed
the world's glory and authority into the least trustworthy of
hands – the devil. This is why the devil could offer them to
Jesus.

The most interesting feature of Luke's account, however,
is, as we noted in the introduction to this chapter, that the
second and third tests are reversed. In Matthew's Gospel the
grand climax is the definitive statement that God and God
alone should be worshipped; in Luke the climax of the whole
story is Jesus' refusal to put God to the test. In Luke, however,
probably more important than Jesus' refusal to test God is
the location of this final test, which is in Jerusalem. Couple
this with Luke's final statement in Luke 4.13 – that the devil
departed from him 'until an opportune time' – and another
feature of Luke's telling of this narrative becomes clear.

In Mark and Matthew, Jesus' testing lasted until the devil
departed; indeed in Matthew Jesus dismissed the devil with
a flourish. In Luke, however, the devil merely left until there
was a good opportunity to return. Luke prepares us, therefore, for other times when the devil would return to test
Jesus once more. Before you begin to wrack your brains for

those moments in Luke when the devil comes back to test Jesus, let me help you out. Although Satan does appear a few times more, it is not to test Jesus. Nevertheless, Jesus *is* tested again and again during his ministry. Luke introduces the intriguing notion that the devil does in fact return in the guise of the various people and groups who often challenged him to leave his calling as the self-giving, suffering Son of God and to make easier, less costly, choices.

Ending the testings in Jerusalem can only remind us of the next time that Jesus will be tested in Jerusalem – in the garden of Gethsemane, in his trial and, most of all, on the cross. Luke balances carefully the acknowledgement of the particular person of the devil (to whom the world and all its glory has been delivered) and the recognition that his accusing, testing role can take many beguiling forms. In doing this, Luke reminds us that Satan does not always arrive obviously bedecked with horns and a trident; diabolical testing can take many different forms, undermining our sense of self and calling until we have forgotten who we really are and who we are called to be.

Luke's challenge is that we should stay alert and be aware that testing still comes in many different forms and can so easily send us spinning off course before we are even aware of its danger.

20

Luke 13.31–35 At that very hour some Pharisees came and said to him, 'Get away from here, for Herod wants to kill you.' He said to them, 'Go and tell that fox for me, "Listen, I am casting out demons and performing cures today and tomorrow, and on the third day I finish my work. Yet today, tomorrow, and the next day I must be on my way, because it is impossible for a prophet to be killed outside of

Jerusalem." Jerusalem, Jerusalem, the city that kills the prophets and stones those who are sent to it! How often have I desired to gather your children together as a hen gathers her brood under her wings, and you were not willing! See, your house is left to you. And I tell you, you will not see me until the time comes when you say, "Blessed is the one who comes in the name of the Lord."'

One of the odder stories in Luke's Gospel is this one in Luke 13. Here Jesus has unusual allies in the shape of the Pharisees who came to warn him that Herod wanted to kill him. At first glance there seems little purpose to this story until you remember those ominous words in Luke 4.13 that the devil had simply departed until 'an opportune time'. This is an interesting example of one of those times. Let me be clear, I am not for a moment suggesting that either the Pharisees or Herod are actually the devil in this story, but what both of them do is to test Jesus in a very similar way to the way the devil tested him in Luke 4.

At the heart of Luke's story, here is the declaration that Jesus had set his face towards Jerusalem (9.51–53). Luke, the author, and we, the readers, both know that his fate in Jerusalem will be his ultimate test – the way of suffering and death. Here the Pharisees, in passing on the unhappy gossip that Herod sought to kill him, raise the question of whether he should flee, leaving his designated path and running for his life. On one level, we might imagine that Jesus could have been tempted by this news. If his ultimate destination needed to be Jerusalem, then might it not have been sensible to listen to this dire warning and take another route in order to reach his final goal?

This is where the parallels between this event and the temptations come to the fore. One of the things that the devil offered Jesus in the wilderness was a shortcut – a quick route to recognition. The miraculous production of bread, authority over the kingdoms of this world and a dramatic angelic rescue from plummeting to his death would all have brought immediate recognition. Here Jesus is offered the shortcut of hurrying onwards to Jerusalem. Jesus declined both forms of shortcut.

His real calling was neither immediate global recognition nor indeed simply arriving in Jerusalem. In the end he achieved both but that was not what he came to do. What he came to do was to cast out demons and heal the sick. It is in fact striking to contrast what Herod 'wanted' with what Jesus 'wanted'. Herod wanted to kill Jesus (13.31); Jesus wanted to gather Jerusalem like a hen gathers her children (13.34). Jesus came to heal, to nurture and to love. Neither the offer of riches and wealth, nor the threat of death, was going to knock him off course. Through thick and thin, Jesus remained faithful to his calling and looked fame and death in the eye with equal equanimity.

As we reflect on the model Jesus offers us, it is important to recognize his clarity in the face of panic and strength in the face of anxiety. Jesus knew what he had come to do and who he was called to be and was not deflected from this no matter how great the temptations. We are called to similar steadfastness. It is so easy to be deflected or tempted from the path we tread by the promise of quick rewards. It is even easier to be frightened off our path by harbingers of doom and disaster. The real challenge is keeping our vision clear no matter what threatens to throw us off course.

21

Luke 23.34–39 Then Jesus said, 'Father, forgive them; for they do not know what they are doing.' And they cast lots to divide his clothing. And the people stood by, watching;

but the leaders scoffed at him, saying, 'He saved others; let him save himself if he is the Messiah of God, his chosen one!' The soldiers also mocked him, coming up and offering him sour wine, and saying, 'If you are the King of the Jews, save yourself!' There was also an inscription over him, 'This is the King of the Jews.' One of the criminals who were hanged there kept deriding him and saying, 'Are you not the Messiah? Save yourself and us!'

Irony is an acquired taste. Some love it; others find it irritating. Personally I love irony as it allows the possibility for in-depth reflection without the need to spell things out. The ironic statement hangs in the air suggesting, questioning and probing without ever needing to state explicitly the range of ideas to which it points. I am fully aware that explaining irony runs close to explaining jokes – you can do it but you will ruin the whole experience – but am going to do so anyway here with due apology to those who will wish I hadn't.

The reason why it is important to explain Luke's irony here is because it so neatly fits with Luke's theme of a testing that runs all the way through the Gospel. Here, as in Luke 4, Jesus is tested three times. Here the testing is prefaced with a challenge about identity ('if he is the Messiah of God', v. 35; 'if you are the king of the Jews', v. 36; 'are you not the Messiah?', v. 39). The challenge about identity is now focused around whether Jesus is the anointed one or king of the Jews, not whether he is the Son of God as in Luke 4, but the underlying question remains the same. Just as in Luke 4, Jesus is challenged to prove his identity by fulfilling the criteria set down for him by other people.

Here Jesus received one test expressed three times (as opposed to the three different tests of Luke 4) which all challenged him to save himself as the proof that he was God's Messiah. This is where the irony kicks in with full force. The irony is that it was precisely *because* he was the Messiah that Jesus refused to save himself. His refusal to save himself *was* what saved us. Just like the devil in Luke 4, the crowd, the soldiers and one of the criminals all 'knew' what being a Messiah entailed. They thought that a real Messiah would prove his power to save by saving himself. Jesus knew, Luke knew and we know that the opposite was the case. The very thing that they thought disproved that he was the Messiah – his suffering and death on a cross – is what demonstrates to us that he was the Messiah. What they believed undermined his ability to save them – his refusal to save himself – was precisely what saved us.

In Jesus' last and greatest test of his life he faced again the siren call of falling in with other people's vision for who he was and what he would do. To paraphrase what the crowd, soldiers and criminal said: 'we will believe in you, if you do what we think you should do'. This siren call echoes as vividly today as it ever did during the time of Jesus. There is no shortage of people who line up to declare what a disciple must be and do; or what the Church must be and do. The challenge we face is how we work out our calling in the face of the loudly clamouring voices all eager to tell us that a 'good disciple' will always do this or that; that a 'good church' will always be this. Sometimes these voices are right but often they are wrong – calling on us to 'save ourselves' as they did to Jesus on the cross.

This is not a counsel to ignore all critique – healthy critique can help us discern the right way forward – but it is a counsel not to be swayed by the voices of those who don't understand your calling. The message that emerges time and time again from Jesus' own testing by the devil is the importance of self-understanding and identity – of knowing who you are and what God has called you to do. Staying true to this is vital. For Jesus, the salvation of the whole world, depended on it, for us the stakes are lower but are, nevertheless, still important.

22

Luke 8.11–15 *Now the parable is this: The seed is the word of God. The ones on the path are those who have heard; then the devil comes and takes away the word from their hearts, so that they may not believe and be saved. The ones on the rock are those who, when they hear the word, receive it with joy. But these have no root; they believe only for a while and in a time of testing fall away. As for what fell among the thorns, these are the ones who hear; but as they go on their way, they are choked by the cares and riches and pleasures of life, and their fruit does not mature. But as for that in the good soil, these are the ones who, when they hear the word, hold it fast in an honest and good heart, and bear fruit with patient endurance.*

Anyone who has ever tried to grow anything can resonate, in one way or another, with the parable of the sower. Whether we've dabbled with growing flowers or herbs, vegetables or fruit, the mystery of the plants that grow and those that don't grow is as puzzling today as it was in the first century. If only it were as simple as it appears in this parable: good soil = good growth. While it is certainly true that sowing on the path, on rocks or among thorns will almost certainly produce no growth (unless you are trying to grow weeds), it is, alas, not the case that sowing in good soil will guarantee good growth. I am often tempted to add in extra potential calamities for the seed that falls on good soil – the seed falls in good soil and grows well but then the slug comes at night and feasts on the seedling until only a stick remains; or a late frost bites, killing everything that had begun to grow; or it rains all summer so nothing can ripen. It is also quite fun to imagine what the slug, frost or rain might be in a modern context. (I have lots of ideas!)

Luke's point, however, is even more pointed than this. When we read this passage against Jesus' testing in the wilderness, the power of the parable is even greater. All of the Gospels associate the devil with the birds who ate the seed from the path (in Matthew he is named the 'evil one' 13.19; and in Mark, 'Satan', 4.15) but Luke alone associates the rocky ground with testing. The word for 'testing' is the same word as was used for Jesus' testing by the devil.

The parable of the sower, it turns out, is the parable of testing. Jesus was tested throughout his life – as we observed in the previous three passages – and Luke's Gospel goes on to note subtly that his disciples must expect to be tested in the same kind of way. We, the seed, need to expect that the devil will be as testing, challenging and exacting of us as he was of Jesus. Given half a chance, the devil would have swooped in and consumed the good seed that was Jesus the Son of God in the wilderness; it was simply that he was not even given half a chance. Jesus ensured that good soil was all that was on offer.

What is particularly interesting in Luke's version of this parable is that Luke identifies the act of testing itself as something that causes a seed sown on rocky ground not to grow. He did not underestimate the difficulties that testing can pose. Jesus – the one whom we follow – was tested and remained firm and sure in his identity. For so many of us, even the act of testing can cause us to wither and die. Jesus stands before us as a model of someone for whom testing was not destructive but clarifying: we know more of who Jesus really was after his testing than before. Testing will not always be destructive but it can be. Only the arrogant and foolish believe they have nothing to fear from being tested.

Luke's parable of the sower looks with sober judgement at the challenge of testing and reminds us of what can happen if that testing loosens our grip on who we really are and what we are called to be and do. Luke, rightly, slaps a big warning sign about testing and its consequences on to his Gospel – a warning that we would do well to heed.

23

Luke 22.28 *You are those who have stood by me in my trials.*

Luke 11.4 *And forgive us our sins, for we ourselves forgive everyone indebted to us. And do not bring us to the time of trial.*

Luke 22.40 *When he reached the place, he said to them, 'Pray that you may not come into the time of trial.'*

In this chapter we have seen how the theme of testing runs all the way through Luke's Gospel. In case we are in any doubt about how important it has been to Luke's narrative about Jesus at the end of his life, Jesus recognized that the disciples had stood by him during his trials. Again the word used here is the word *peirasmos*, the same one used of the devil's encounter with Jesus, and the same one, as we will see below, that we pray every time we pray the Lord's prayer. At the last supper, then, Jesus commended the disciples for staying with him through the many experiences that he designated as 'testing' during his ministry.

As we all know, it was just as well he thanked them at that point since when the real 'testing' came they were nowhere to be seen. It is in recognition of the true difficulty of testing that when they left the last supper and went to the garden of Gethsemane, Jesus urged them to pray that they might not come to a time of testing. While he went away to pray his own prayer in the face of his biggest and most difficult 'test', the disciples were overcome with sleep and did not pray as Jesus suggested. Whether their prayer would have made any difference in any case is a moot point – the tide of events had already turned and Jesus' death was as good as inevitable – nevertheless, the disciples did not pray that they be saved from a time of testing; they went to sleep instead, and so when the test came, somewhat unsurprisingly, they failed utterly – running away and, in Peter's case, denying Jesus three times.

It is this context in Luke that suggests that we should think long and hard about Jesus' command in the Lord's Prayer that we pray, in the translation of the NRSV, that we are not brought into a time of trial (or, more literally, 'that we are not brought into testing'). The same phrase appears in Matthew's version of the Lord's Prayer, but with even more punch – there we are to pray that we will not be brought into testing but will be rescued from the 'evil one'. The reason Jesus tells us to pray like this is because he, of all people, knows how hard it is to stand firm in the face of testing and to remain true to your calling. Better, far better, for us not to need to stand true at all because the testing has passed us by.

Realistically, however, no matter how fervently we pray, testing will come our way just as it came Jesus' way too. There is no avoiding times of testing – times when who we really are is put to the test. Jesus knew this and, I suspect, that his command to pray that we are not brought to testing is as much about preparing us for what such times ask of us as it is a realistic expectation that we can avoid testing altogether. When we are totally unprepared and are blindsided by the testing (as the disciples were in the garden of Gethsemane) it is far, far harder to stand firm than it is when we are ready.

The Lord's Prayer, if we pray it with minds alert, reminds us of the danger of testing and of how easy it is, despite our very best intentions, to crumble under the testing and not to be true to the person that God has called us to be and the behaviour that this requires of us.

At the same time, it is worth reminding ourselves that we follow Jesus but are not Jesus. Jesus was able to stand firm and true not only during his testing by the devil but throughout his ministry – even on the cross he knew who he was called to be and what he was called to do. Inevitably, although we aim to emulate him as far as we can, we will fail and, like the disciples, fall asleep, run away and deny him. This is where Luke's narrative picks us up, dusts us down and reminds us of forgiveness. The disciples were forgiven and so will we be. It is best to avoid testing at all. Next best is to stand firm and true in the face of testing, but it is also all right to fail and be forgiven – this, after all, is the heart of the gospel.

Testing is a part of life. It was certainly a part of Jesus' life. Luke's reflective narrative on testing brings us to the recognition that testing can take many different forms and take place at many different times in our lives. It does not conveniently come clearly packaged with a label 'testing by the devil'. Sometimes it will be very obviously so, but often requires the skill of discernment and reflection to identify the nature of the testing and what the right response to it should be. The dangerous kind of testing by its very nature seeks to knock us off course, to make us less the person God wants us to be, and less sure of our ability to be that person.

Praying 'do not bring us into testing' in the right spirit teaches us an appropriate dread of being tested, a dread that challenges us to acknowledge that sometimes testing will ask of us more than we are able to give. In those times, it is worth remembering the disciples and the transformative power of forgiveness. No matter how hard we pray the Lord's Prayer, testing will come and there will be times when, despite everything, we find ourselves unable to stand firm – but then so did the very first disciples and they went on to achieve great things for God.

Questions for discussion and reflection

Reflecting on Scripture

- Read Luke 4.1–13, then 23.34–39, and then say the Lord's Prayer together.
- Spend a minute or two in silence reflecting on what you heard.
- What themes jumped out for you from these readings? What did they make you think about?

Discuss

On knowing yourself

- At the heart of all of these passages lies the need to know who we are and what God has called us to do and be. Jesus knew. How do we become more confident in knowing this ourselves?
- Now, as then, people love to tell us what being 'us' should mean (what a church should be; how a Christian should behave). Have you had any experiences of this?
- Why do you think it is so tempting to tell other people how to be them? How do we resist such advice when it is offered to us?
- When does steadfastness in the face of challenge tip into being down-right obstinate and refusing to listen to other people's opinions? How do you discern when you need to hold fast and when you need to listen and change? Can we learn anything from Jesus about this?

Testing

- Think about the times in your life when you have been most tested – would you in any way agree with Luke and see these as a testing by the devil? What is helpful about seeing them that way and what is unhelpful?

- Why does 'testing' stop the seed sown in rocky ground from growing? How is this different for seeds grown in 'good soil'? How can we ensure that our roots go deep?

- Why do *you* think Jesus tells us to pray that we are not brought to a time of testing?

- How can we best prepare ourselves to withstand the testing when it comes?

5

FOLLOW ME ...
The Call to Discipleship

In Matthew and Mark, almost the first thing that Jesus did after his testing by the devil was to call Simon and Andrew, James and John to follow him. In Luke, he preached a sermon in the Capernaum synagogue first and then called Simon, James and John to follow him. An essential part of Jesus' ministry was calling disciples and being a Rabbi for them in their learning. In fact, I don't think it is stating it too strongly to say that disciples were essential to Jesus' ministry. According to the Gospel accounts, at least, there was very little of Jesus' ministry spent without disciples. In Matthew and Mark especially, Jesus left the wilderness, moved to Galilee, began to proclaim the Kingdom and immediately called disciples.

Jesus' calling of disciples invariably took the form of an invitation to 'follow'. Following Jesus was how they became his disciples in the first place. It was how their learning took place. It was how Jesus taught them to look outwards and fish for people. Following Jesus is a step into a momentous adventure with Jesus, an adventure marked by everything we can learn from him.

The first few reflections in this chapter will be based on the calling of Simon Peter, Andrew, James and John as in previous chapters, you might find it helpful to read the whole passage before we begin, both from Matthew and from Luke:

Matthew 4.17–23 *From that time Jesus began to proclaim, 'Repent, for the kingdom of heaven has come near.' As he walked by the Sea of Galilee, he saw two brothers, Simon, who is called Peter, and Andrew his brother, casting a net into the lake – for they were fishermen. And he said to them, 'Follow me, and I will make you fish for people.' Immediately they left their nets and followed him. As he went from there, he saw two other brothers, James son of Zebedee and his brother John, in the boat with their father Zebedee, mending their nets, and he called them. Immediately they left the boat and their father, and followed him. Jesus went throughout Galilee, teaching in their synagogues and proclaiming the good news of the kingdom and curing every disease and every sickness among the people.*

Luke 5.1–11 *Once while Jesus was standing beside the lake of Gennesaret, and the crowd was pressing in on him to hear the word of God, he saw two boats there at the shore of the lake; the fishermen had gone out of them and were washing their nets. He got into one of the boats, the one belonging to Simon, and asked him to put out a little way from the shore. Then he sat down and taught the crowds from the boat. When he had finished speaking, he said to Simon, 'Put out into the deep water and let down your nets for a catch.' Simon answered, 'Master, we have worked all night long but have caught nothing. Yet if you say so, I will let down the nets.' When they had done this, they caught so many fish that their nets were beginning to break. So they signalled to their partners in the other boat to come and help them. And they came and filled both boats, so that they began to sink. But when Simon Peter saw it, he fell down at Jesus' knees, saying, 'Go away from me, Lord, for I am a sinful man!' For he and all who were with him were amazed at the catch of fish that they had taken; and so also were James and John, sons of Zebedee, who were partners* *with Simon. Then Jesus said to Simon, 'Do not be afraid; from now on you will be catching people.' When they had brought their boats to shore, they left everything and followed him.*

24

Matthew 4.19–22 *And he said to them, 'Follow me, and I will make you fish for people.' Immediately they left their nets and followed him. As he went from there, he saw two other brothers, James son of Zebedee and his brother John, in the boat with their father Zebedee, mending their nets, and he called them. Immediately they left the boat and their father, and followed him.*

Teachers have always identified talented students and encouraged them to learn further. I've done it myself. In the course of teaching it quickly becomes clear that there are people who have the capacity to enjoy learning more. Many teachers then sidle up to these people and look for ways to encourage them to continue on to the next stage. Rabbis were no different. Later Jewish texts talk about the way that Rabbis identified bright, talented students (or *talmidim* in Hebrew) and invited them to learn with them.

You could say that this was exactly what Jesus was doing here, apart from one key difference. The Rabbi–disciple relationship was normally shaped around recognizing the talent of someone who was intent on studying Jewish law and inviting them to leave home and travel with the Rabbi in order to learn both how that Rabbi understood the law and how this affected the way he – they always were 'he' at this point – saw the world in which he lived. In other words, disciples were normally students already, who were seeking new and greater challenges. They were often identified as bright students, destined to go far. They might have a choice of a number of Rabbis with whom to learn. Being a disciple was probably something they planned and fitted well with the life they had chosen.

The striking feature of this call passage is that there is nothing in the text to suggest that Simon Peter, Andrew, James and John were looking for a Rabbi from whom to learn. They were fishing: engaged in their everyday lives, working at their trade; for all we know they expected to do this for the rest of their lives. The invitation from Jesus to be disciples, therefore, would have turned their lives upside down. When they followed him they left their lives, their livelihood, their family and all their expectations behind.[9]

I am often asked how I got to be where I am. The question is often couched in terms that imply that I sat down at the age of eight and made a life-plan which I have followed rigidly ever since. The reality is quite different. I have, as far as anyone can, tried to live my life open to the calling of Jesus. This might make it sound straightforward and as though the calling has always been clear – like that of Jesus to Simon Peter. It wasn't. It might also make it sound as though I think I have succeeded. I haven't. I have lived through long periods of time when the cloud has been down and I have no idea of the next step, but eventually the cloud does lift and little by little the next step emerges, and then the next one. It is shaky, uncertain and vague – but following step by step has brought me to places I could never have planned for. I often look backwards on my life with vague bemusement and forwards with complete blankness. I did not plan to be where I am, so I simply could not tell you

---

9 It is probably worth noting that the impression of 'leaving everything' given in this story is somewhat diluted by later stories that talk about Simon Peter's care for his mother-in-law and the easy access to boats that Jesus and his disciples had. Nevertheless, following Jesus would have turned the expected course of their lives on their heads.

where I will be in five, ten or fifteen years. There is no plan. My only plan, shaky though it sounds, is to be as faithful as it is possible to be to the one calling.

This leads me to wonder what it felt like for those first disciples to leave everything they knew and step out behind the one who simply says 'follow me'. Did they know the enormity of what they were doing when they left their nets? Did they have any idea that in a few decades they would be travelling through the known world, proclaiming the Kingdom to everyone they met? The fact that they followed at all suggests that they had no idea what responding meant. They did what so many of us have done. Jesus called and they followed. It made no sense at all; it made all the sense in the world. Following Jesus involves tearing up your life-plan and throwing it to the wind; following Jesus may change everything about your life, or just some of it; following Jesus summons you to the biggest adventure of your life. It is hard, uncertain, often vague and unformed, and the most satisfying thing you will ever do.

$\mathscr{D}$

25

Matthew 4.19 *And he said to them, 'Follow me, and I will make you fish for people.'*

I wonder what the word 'learn' conjures up for you? We are blessed in the west in the twenty-first century with an effective and far-reaching education system. Most of us will have spent around 15 years (and in some of our cases much longer than that) in full-time 'learning'. I am someone who has benefited hugely from this education system and I am regularly, profoundly thankful for it. The slight difficulty with it, however, is that it causes us to assume that formal, taught 'learning' is the only learning that takes place. As a result, when we look at the Gospels we look for occasions when Jesus was speaking and assume that this is all the 'teaching of Jesus', and that the disciples, learning took place only in this context.

The reality is that the disciples learnt in a wide variety of ways. Of course they learnt when Jesus spoke. They also learnt by following him, by asking questions and more questions, by watching what he did and how he interacted with others, by getting things wrong and needing to ask again. The disciples learnt from Jesus in a large number of different ways; sitting down and listening to him 'teach' was only one of many others.

In the context of this, Jesus' words to Simon Peter and Andrew are striking. He did not say 'follow me and I will teach you how to emulate me' or 'follow me and I will communicate everything you need to know' or 'follow me and your walk in the way of the Lord will be transformed'. In fact, he doesn't say, at all, what we might expect him to say. What he says is outward facing, challenging and intriguing.

Jesus' declaration 'I will make you fish for people' has, as many will know, a much more pleasing pun in the King James Version (and those versions that follow it like the Revised Standard Version (RSV); English Standard Version (ESV); and the New American Standard Version (NAS)); speaking to fishermen he says, 'I will make you fishers of men'. The problem of course is that in the language of the twenty-first century this implies that Simon Peter and Andrew will seek only male disciples which the entirety of Jesus' ministry illustrates was not what he meant. Galling as it is to lose such a good pun, it may make you feel better to know the pun only works in English and is not implied in the Greek, which literally translated reads 'I will make you fishermen of people'.

Jesus' call then is to learning – making them fish for people implies a level of training – but it is learning with an active outcome. This begs the questions of what fishing for people entails. Jeremiah 16.16 talks about sending for fishermen (and hunters) to catch sinful people so they can be judged (the image is used similarly in Amos 4.2 and Habakkuk 1.14–17). It is worth remembering that a fishing image is also combined with judgement in Matthew 13.47–50 where the fish are separated into good and bad baskets. In popular contexts the Englush word 'judge' is used to imply that the judgement will be a negative one. In the New Testament this is not always the case. Judgement is not necessarily bad. Sometimes it is and sometimes it is not, as the parable from Matthew 13 indicates. It may be better then to use the word 'decision' of the event: the disciples are to bring people to a moment of decision when they and God decide who they really are.

The learning of discipleship, then, is true learning but it is learning for action. It is all too easy to see learning as being for our own benefit, to make us a better people. This is not what Jesus summoned Simon Peter and Andrew to. Jesus summoned them to action for the Kingdom, to join him in proclaiming repentance and the forgiveness of sins, and to bring people to a crucial moment of decision. We are not called to be disciples for our sakes but for the Kingdom's sake. As we fish we learn untold riches about ourselves, God, the world he created and the Kingdom. As disciples we follow Jesus and, as we do so, we learn and learn and learn, but this is not why we become disciples in the first place.

26

Luke 5.1–3 and 7 *Once while Jesus was standing beside the lake of Gennesaret, and the crowd was pressing in on him to hear the word of God, he saw two boats there at the shore of the lake; the fishermen had gone out of them and were washing their nets. He got into one of the boats, the one belonging to Simon. So they signalled to their partners in the other boat to come and help them.*

Mark 1.20 *Immediately he called them; and they left their father Zebedee in the boat with the hired men, and followed him.*

John 12.20–22 *Now among those who went up to worship at the festival were some Greeks. They came to Philip, who was from Bethsaida in Galilee, and said to him, 'Sir, we wish to see Jesus.' Philip went and told Andrew; then Andrew and Philip went and told Jesus.*

You may be wondering why I have included this slightly odd collection of verses together here. The reason is because I want to tackle head on the assumption that the disciples, especially the first four, were poor, simple, uneducated fishermen. It is widely accepted – and regularly stated – that the disciples are ignorant, labouring types with little education between them. Peter is often described as a 'simple fisherman' but a simple fisherman couldn't have written Greek as good as that.[10]

In fairness we are fed this line in Acts 4.13 which talks about the rulers of the people to whom Peter and John spoke realizing 'that they were uneducated and ordinary men'. This perception is enhanced by the King James Version which translates this as 'unlearned and ignorant' men, though the word translated as 'ignorant' really just means 'lay' or 'non-specialist', and 'unlearned' is probably in this context not trained in the minutiae of the law. In other words, the rulers of the people were prejudiced against these Galilean tradespeople who were not Jerusalem-trained experts in Torah, and were amazed with the wisdom and boldness of what

10 For more on the social status of Simon Peter, Andrew, James, see the wonderful article by Jerome Murphy O'Connor 'Fishers of fish, fishers of men' *Bible Review* 15/3 (1999), pp. 22–7 and 48–9.

they said. Rather sadly, Christian tradition has accepted, unchallenged, this prejudice and peddled it for the past 2,000 years.

The evidence from the Gospels suggests that Simon Peter, Andrew, James and John were far from 'poor, simple, trades-people'. Fish was big business at the time of Jesus and demand for it far outstripped supply, so much so that in Rome a fish was said to sell for far more than a cow. We also know, from Luke 5.7, that the families of Peter and Andrew, James and John were in partnership and, from Mark 1.20, that the Zebedee family had employees or hired hands. The archaeological remains of what is commonly agreed to be Simon Peter's house in Capernaum indicate that it is much bigger than most other houses in the town.

A final but fascinating detail comes from John's Gospel, which talks about Greeks wanting to meet Jesus, and Philip going to Andrew before approaching Jesus. The implication of this is that Andrew was also a Greek speaker. The likelihood being that he had learned to speak Greek in order to trade fish more effectively in Galilee. There is little to suggest that Peter, Andrew, James and John fitted, in any way, our stereotype of them – it is much more likely that they were highly successful business owners able to speak both Aramaic and Greek.

This does not in any way undermine the fact that Jesus came for the lost and least of our world. Many, many stories throughout the Gospels give testimony to this. What it does is challenge our assumptions that 'ordinary' people are 'simple and ignorant'. Then as now, ordinary people bring a wealth of experience: some are trained, others untrained; some scrape by making a living, others are successfully engaged in business; some are wealthy, others poor. In the Kingdom of God no one is to be written off as 'simple and ignorant'; all are loved and embraced for who they are and the gifts they bring to us. If Christian tradition has been so wrong for so long about Peter, Andrew, James and John, just think how much danger we are in when we make sweeping assumptions about people today.

27

***Matthew 9.9** As Jesus was walking along, he saw a man called Matthew sitting at the tax booth; and he said to him, 'Follow me.' And he got up and followed him.*

Of Jesus' earliest followers, the five we know most about are Simon Peter, Andrew, James, John and Matthew (or Levi),[11] since these five were engaged in their jobs before being called by Jesus. If Simon Peter, Andrew, James and John were highly respectable businessmen, Matthew was the opposite. The widespread contemporary view of tax collectors is illustrated simply with the phrase 'tax collectors and sinners' (Matthew 9.9). The question of precisely who the sinners were has been debated extensively – after all there is no role description 'sinner' as there is 'tax collector' – but most agree that the 'sinners' were those whose relationship with the law and/ or the temple placed them permanently on the outskirts of society. That 'sinners' were cited alongside tax collectors also indicates that tax collectors found themselves in a similar position.

Then as now taxes were charged on a wide range of different items. There was a harvest tax levied on landowners; there was a property tax levied on those who owned slaves,

---

11 The account in Mark 2.14 and Luke 5.27 is so similar to the calling of Matthew here that scholars conclude that Matthew/Levi were the same person and had two names. The argument that Levi is his Hebrew name and Matthew his Greek (a bit like Saul/Paul) doesn't work as *Mattiya* is the Hebrew of the Greek *Mattaios*. Either, then, he had two Hebrew names or Matthew was given to him by Jesus (meaning 'gift of the Lord').

cattle and buildings and, of importance here, a trade tax levied on goods transported across borders. Matthew, sitting at a tax booth in Capernaum, clearly collected this latter tax. Capernaum at the time of Jesus was a bustling international commercial centre on both the north–south and east–west trade routes; it was the last town in Galilee before Bethsaida, in the area ruled by Herod Philip, and so the tax booth existed to levy a fee on goods carried between Galilee and Iturea.

Much has been said in the past about the corruption of tax collectors due to a system called 'tax farming' where tax collectors bought a licence to levy tax and then set whatever rates they chose to recoup (and profit from) the fee. However, this was outlawed as a practice by the Emperor Augustus and no longer allowed during the time of Jesus. The only corruption available to a tax collector during the time of Jesus would have been in over-estimating the amount of goods transported. The roots of the hatred towards the tax collectors are more likely to be found not in their corruption but in the fact that they were Roman collaborators mixing daily with Gentiles (and that no one has ever liked tax collectors).

What is striking about the story is that there were, the story implies, a good number of tax collectors around (the trade route through Capernaum probably required a lot of them) who appear to be used to dining together: the tax collectors and sinner came and joined Jesus and Matthew as they ate (Matthew 9.10). They were outcasts from wider society but seem to have formed a bond between themselves as a result. I have been in a number of places where the bond formed between people who feel like fellow 'outsiders' is deeper and richer than any of the bonds between the 'insiders'. Uncomfortable though being an 'outsider' is, the richness of the relationship you form with other 'outsiders' is noteworthy.

Jesus' calling to Matthew was a calling to inclusion back into a world from which he had been cast out. His following of Jesus allowed him to relate to people outside of his small, excluded world. The contrast between him and Simon Peter, Andrew, James and John is, on the surface, stark. The four fishermen had much to lose; Matthew had much to gain. In reality, the losing and the gaining probably evened out. The fishermen lost the stability and status of their business; Matthew lost the close camaraderie of a group of fellow outsiders. Matthew gained a breadth of relationship impossible to him before and so did the fishermen.

Following Jesus is both costly and a priceless gift. Following Jesus costs us everything; following Jesus provides us with untold riches of experience, learning and relationship. Sometimes those who feel they have less to lose can see the benefits more clearly than those whose vision is clouded with what they feel they need to hold on to. To quote from the New English Bible translation of the Beatitudes 'How blest are those who know their need of God' (Matthew 5.3), for without this knowledge of our need of God the cost can sometimes feel too great to bear.

28

Luke 9.57–62 As they were going along the road, someone said to him, 'I will follow you wherever you go.' And Jesus said to him, 'Foxes have holes, and birds of the air have nests; but the Son of Man has nowhere to lay his head.' To another he said, 'Follow me.' But he said, 'Lord, first let me go and bury my father.' But Jesus said to him, 'Let the dead bury their own dead; but as for you, go and proclaim the kingdom of God.' Another said, 'I will follow you, Lord; but let me first say farewell to those at my home.' Jesus said to him, 'No one who puts a hand to the plough and looks back is fit for the kingdom of God.'

Mark 10.21–22 *Jesus, looking at him, loved him and said, 'You lack one thing; go, sell what you own, and give the money to the poor, and you will have treasure in heaven; then come, follow me.' When he heard this, he was shocked and went away grieving, for he had many possessions.*

In the previous passage we began to touch on the cost of discipleship, but in these two passages the cost hits us between the eyes with full force. The passage from Luke contains three conversations between Jesus and potential disciples. The passage from Mark comes from the end of a conversation between Jesus and a man who wanted to know what he had to do to inherit eternal life, and although his question was not directly about discipleship it has a similar edge to it.

Even the scholars who are the most sceptical about what we can know Jesus did or did not actually say agree that he must have said these words in Luke 9.57–62 (and their equivalent Matthew 8.19–22). This is simply because they are so rude that no one would have made them up. If you were creating a narrative about your leader you would not choose for him to say this. This also suggests that he must have said these kinds of things quite often so that no one felt able to leave them out. Despite vast efforts made on many people's part, there is no real way to make these demands less offensive. They *are* offensive and I suspect Jesus intended them to be offensive.

The way into reflecting on them, that I have found most helpful is through the most difficult and bemusing one of all: 'Let the dead bury their own dead'. Surely, by definition, that is an impossibility? One solution is to assume that Jesus meant the spiritually dead should bury the physically dead, though that involves reading quite a lot into the passage. The solution that makes most sense to me, however, refers back to Jewish burial practice. People were buried very quickly due to the heat but then after a year, during which the family would have mourned, their bones would have been moved to an alcove along with the bones of the rest of the ancestors. The request to wait until the father had been buried might well have been a request to wait up to a year.

The person who wanted to say goodbye to his family was someone who came up to Jesus to say 'I will follow you but…!' His moment of decision was clouded by things he needed to do first. In other words, these passages, including the one from Mark, are all about excuses: 'I will follow you… but could it be comfortable and convenient?'; 'I will follow you … in about a year's time'; 'I will follow you … but first let me do something else'; 'I want eternal life AND all my stuff'.

Jesus' uncompromising – even rude – answer is that the way of the Kingdom is costly. Following Jesus involves discomfort and dislocation. Following cannot be slotted on top of already existing commitments. Following requires everything from us. There should be no qualifiers after the statement 'I will follow you'. Jesus is not interested in 'I will follow but …' or 'I will follow, can I just …?'

Jesus still calls to us 'Come, follow me'. Whether we hear that call for the first time, or after many years of following, the challenge for each one of us is what gets in the way of this for us? Family? Time constraints? Our belongings? Just like the would-be followers of these passages, we still add phrases on to the end of our response: 'I will follow you but…' They may be different excuses but we still make them

29

John 1.35–46 *The next day John again was standing with two of his disciples, and as he watched Jesus walk by, he exclaimed, 'Look, here is the Lamb of God!' The two disciples heard him say this, and they followed Jesus. When Jesus turned and saw them following, he said to them, 'What are you looking for?' They said to him, 'Rabbi' (which translated means Teacher), 'where are you staying?' He said to them, 'Come and see.' They came and saw where he was staying, and they remained with him that day. It was about four o' clock in the afternoon. One of the two who heard John speak and followed him was Andrew, Simon Peter's brother. He first found his brother Simon and said to him, 'We have found the Messiah' (which is translated Anointed). He brought Simon to Jesus, who looked at him and said, 'You are Simon son of John. You are to be called Cephas' (which is translated Peter). The next day Jesus decided to go to Galilee. He found Philip and said to him, 'Follow me.' Now Philip was from Bethsaida, the city of Andrew and Peter. Philip found Nathanael and said to him, 'We have found him about whom Moses in the law and also the prophets wrote, Jesus son of Joseph from Nazareth.' Nathanael said to him, 'Can anything good come out of Nazareth?' Philip said to him, 'Come and see.'*

The startling feature of the account of the call of the disciples in Matthew, Mark and Luke is that they give us no indication as to why the disciples were prepared to leave their boats or tax booths, or in fact anything else, to follow Jesus. Jesus appeared, summoned them and off they went. We are left to assume that there was something about Jesus' message or persona that was so commanding that the disciples had no choice but to follow him. Matthew, Mark and Luke tell the story as it might have appeared to someone watching and has within it the hint of bemusement and surprise you might feel at the sudden leaving of their old life for a new one.

John's Gospel shows us another side of what I would see as the same story. From John's Gospel we learn that Andrew had already felt the 'divine itch': that sense that there is something in us that cannot be satisfied by anything our current life offers. C. S. Lewis described it as 'a desire that nothing in this world can satisfy'; St Augustine describes it as our hearts being restless until they find their rest in God. This 'itch' nags and nags at us until, driven to distraction, we go in search of something with which to scratch it. Sometimes we can find temporary respite from the itch – through work, partying, travelling, you name it we look for it – but ultimately the respite we need can only be found when we find the way to rest in God, to follow his Son, Jesus, and to be refreshed by the Spirit. The divine itch is what draws us to God in the first place but it never really stops. Even once we have heard and responded to God's call of love, the itch comes again and again, calling us back into his embrace, summoning us deeper into faith in him and driving us onwards in striving for the Kingdom.

John's account is an account of divine itchiness. Andrew, it appears, had already felt that itch which was why he, and another unnamed disciple, had become disciples of John the Baptist. In John's Gospel Andrew had already begun his search, a search that reached its end point in his encounter with Jesus, but he wasn't the only one. The language John uses implies that not only Andrew, but also Simon Peter, Philip, and even the sceptical Nathanael, quickly recognized that Jesus was 'the one' – the scratch to their itch. This account of Jesus' calling of disciples reveals that deep-down recognition, the sense of homecoming and profound relief, that always accompanies the meeting of the one for whom you have waited.

So which is the right account, the moment of sudden

inexplicable decision of Matthew, Mark and Luke or the slow burning itch of John? The answer is, of course, both. Decisions often appear to others as a sudden, surprising moment of clarity when most often – though not always – they are a culmination of restlessness and searching. The key is to be people who are attuned to our sense of divine restlessness, who live in and through it, who don't try to ignore it but find out where it is taking us so that, when the moment of clarity suddenly comes upon us, we can see it for what it is and jump up ready for the next adventure with the one who rarely tells us where we are going but does promise that he will be with us on the way.

Today just as much as in the first century Jesus continues to call 'come, follow me'. Now, as much as ever, his call invites us to throw our carefully planned lives in the air and to set out on a grand adventure of love, declaring that no one is too unimportant or too untouchable, summoning people to come and see, drawing them to that moment of recognition and decision when they can at last acknowledge that Jesus is indeed the scratch to their itch, the fulfilment of their restless desire, their homecoming. Now, as then, the adventure demands our all … and more. Now, as then, following that call is well worth the cost it requires of us.

Questions for discussion and reflection

Reflecting on Scripture

- Read Luke 5.1–11 and John 1.36–46.
- Leave a pause between each of the readings and then spend a minute or two in silence reflecting on what you heard.
- What themes jumped out for you from these readings? In particular, what did you notice about the similarity and difference between the callings?

Discuss

On being called to follow

I have been a Christian all my life, but I can trace significant moments when the call to follow (or not follow) has been stronger than at other times; other people have clear moments when they heard that call.

- Do you have a moment or moments when you have felt Jesus' call to follow more strongly than at other times? What was it like? And where did it take you?
- In our busy lives it can be hard to keep on listening for that call to follow; how do you think we can best stay alert to Jesus' call on our lives?
- Talk about Simon Peter, Andrew, James and John – the text suggests they left everything to follow (and yet also does talk later about their families and their use of boats); how disruptive do you think Jesus' call really was on their lives? And is there anything for us to learn from this?
- What has following Jesus meant for you?

Learning from Jesus

- The disciples learnt from Jesus simply by spending

time with him; what kind of things can we do that involve simply 'spending time' in the presence of Jesus?

- What do you think 'fishing for people' means? How might we do it best today?

Fishermen and tax collectors

- Does it make any difference to your mental image of Simon Peter, Andrew, James and John if they were more middle-class business people than improverished workers?

- Talk about what the fishermen gave up to follow Jesus and what Matthew gave up. Was one harder than the other? Have you had to give up anything in your following?

- What are our excuses today that stop us following Jesus as we might? What do we add on to the end of the sentence 'I will follow you but …'

The divine itch

- Have you ever had a 'divine itch' – that sense of restlessness; desire for something beyond yourself; a sense you had to do something but didn't quite know why? Don't worry if the answer is no! But if it's yes, what did you or *should* you do about it?

6

IF YOU WANT TO FOLLOW...
The Character and Cost of Discipleship

Jesus never really declared what kind of people he hoped his disciples might be, and we are left to surmise whether the disciples he got were the disciples he had in mind. Mark's Gospel, at least, hints strongly that the disciples did not, to put it mildly, always fully understand who Jesus was and what he was talking about. This picture came to a head with Peter at Caesarea Philippi when, having finally acknowledged that Jesus was the Messiah, Peter took Jesus aside to rebuke him for suggesting that this meant he would die. Peter had strikingly got it both right and wrong – he recognized who Jesus really was, but then took it upon himself to tell Jesus what this meant.

The disciples in Mark seem often to be on the cusp of true learning and recognition, but never completely there. The factor to bear in mind as we read Mark in the next few sections is that Mark knew, and almost certainly his audience also knew, that Jesus' disciples were now filled by the Spirit and proclaiming the good news of Jesus Christ Son of God to the ends of the earth. They may not have begun as well as we might have hoped, but this didn't stop them later.

Mark's tale of discipleship is one that I find incredibly comforting. The disciples that Jesus chose may not have been the ones we would have chosen, but they were the ones he chose. Were they the ones he had in mind? Quite possibly because, later, they demonstrated that they had done what disciples need to do – they had learned. If they could, so can I and so can you. Being a good disciple is not about being perfect from the outset, but is about being someone who can learn. Perfect I can't do, learning I can.

As this story unfolds we learn something about the character and cost of discipleship. As Jesus sought to draw the disciples onwards into ever-deeper learning from him, he revealed more and more not about what disciples 'do', but about who disciples are. Lessons that are as important today as they were then.

30

Mark 4.35–41 *On that day, when evening had come, he said to them, 'Let us go across to the other side.' And leaving the crowd behind, they took him with them in the boat, just as he was. Other boats were with him. A great gale arose, and the waves beat into the boat, so that the boat was already being swamped. But he was in the stern, asleep on the cushion; and they woke him up and said to him, 'Teacher, do you not care that we are perishing?' He woke up and rebuked the wind, and said to the sea, 'Peace! Be still!' Then the wind ceased, and there was a dead calm. He said to them, 'Why are you afraid? Have you still no faith?' And they were filled with great awe and said to one another, 'Who then is this, that even the wind and the sea obey him?'*

The more you read the Gospels, the easier it is to see the skill and care with which the writers wove their story of Jesus. Of course they were recounting to us what they had seen of Jesus or heard about him, but each one of them did so with insight and skill so that we, the readers, can be drawn into the story and meet Jesus Christ, Son of God, for ourselves. The more I read Mark the more impressed I am by his very careful placing of accounts and provocative statements, which all appear designed to encourage us to reflect deeply about who Jesus was and how we should respond to him.

The second section of Mark's Gospel, which runs from chapter 4 and as far as chapter 8, has as its focus the disciples and their on-going relationship with Jesus. In this section three episodes stand out: the stilling of the storm, at the start of the section in 4.35–41; Jesus' walking on water, right in the middle of the section in 6.47–53; and a final one, a conversation about the leaven of the Pharisees, in 8.13–21. In other words, this section is framed with important conversations between Jesus and his disciples, with another one right in the middle. Two features link each one of these conversations: they all took place in a boat and they all happened while 'crossing over to the other side'. The 'crossing over' detail is important since crossing over to the other side happens often in Mark (4.35; 5.1; 5.21; 6.45; and 8.13) and, when it does, signals an opportunity for learning and transformation.

Mark is signalling to us, therefore, that we are to pay close attention to these conversations – they are an opportunity for travelling to new ways of thinking and the conversations themselves reveal something of what Jesus expected from his disciples.

This first conversation took place after the stilling of the storm. When reading the NRSV translation on this story I often feel really quite sorry for the disciples: they thought they were going to drown and woke Jesus in a fit of terror only for him to ask them why they were afraid. It seems really quite obvious why this was – they thought they were going to die. Imminent death would do it for me. Jesus appears entirely unable to empathize with his disciples.

The passage makes more sense when you realize that the

word translated as 'fear' in verse 40 is not the usual word for fear in Greek. The usual word for fear is *phobos,* from which we get our English words associated with phobia. But in verse 40 Jesus used a different word and hence said something more like 'Why are you so timid?' The Greek word is *deilos* and means something closer to cowardly or fearful rather than just 'fear'. Jesus then links this to faith. This all suggests that the outworking of faith – placing our trust in the one who is ultimately trustworthy – is that we will be less timid, cowardly or fearful. One of the key characteristics of discipleship is that disciples are not timid – thrown around by a mass of fear and foreboding.

I often wonder what our churches, and indeed we ourselves as Christians, might look like if we learnt to be less timid. Much of the conversations I hear in church circles are fear-driven. We are, apparently, constantly terrified by the waves of modern culture, convinced that our ship – the Church – is going to sink into oblivion. I strongly suspect that Jesus might say to us exactly what he said to his first disciples – 'why are you so timid? Have you still no faith?'

31

Mark 6.45–53 *Immediately he made his disciples get into the boat and go on ahead to the other side, to Bethsaida, while he dismissed the crowd. After saying farewell to them, he went up on the mountain to pray. When evening came, the boat was out on the lake, and he was alone on the land. When he saw that they were straining at the oars against an adverse wind, he came towards them early in the morning, walking on the lake. He intended to pass them by. But when they saw him walking on the lake, they thought it was a ghost and cried out; for they all saw him* *and were terrified. But immediately he spoke to them and said, 'Take heart, it is I; do not be afraid.' Then he got into the boat with them and the wind ceased. And they were utterly astounded, for they did not understand about the loaves, but their hearts were hardened. When they had crossed over, they came to land at Gennesaret and moored the boat.*

The second boat episode, in chapter 6, is in some ways similar to the previous boat episode, and in other ways similar to the following one (in chapter 8). The similarity to the stilling of the storm is evident. Again the disciples are crossing the lake, again a wind whipped up, and again with Jesus' presence the wind ceased. The similarity with the following boat episode lies in the fact that both follow on from a miraculous feeding: in chapter 6 five thousand were fed and in chapter 8 four thousand were fed; and in both episodes the disciples did not understand.

The linking of the episodes in this way suggests that we are meant to notice a development, maybe an improvement, that these 'learners' of Jesus have actually learnt something. It turns out that they haven't learnt anything. They were as timid as the last time, though this time Jesus did not comment on this. For those of you who are wondering what word Jesus used for fear here, it is the normal one this time in verb form (*phobeo*), though it is interesting to notice that at the beginning of this phrase he said 'take heart' or 'be of good courage'. The timid disciples still needed Jesus' reassurance and comfort.

As though to compound this lack of progress, Mark tells us that after Jesus got into the boat they were 'utterly astounded'. Actually what Mark says is much stronger even than that. He used two adverbs – greatly and excessively – and then the word which can either be translated as 'amazed' or 'out of one's mind' (it is used this way in Mark 3.31). In other words, the disciples were beside themselves. They were gobsmacked, bamboozled, knocked for six, to suggest just a few possible renderings of these words. This was, Mark tells us, because they did not 'understand about the loaves but their hearts were hardened'.

On one level this feels a little harsh. Jesus had, after all, just walked on the water – surely they were allowed a moment or two of amazement? I suspect the point that Mark was making here can be drawn out of the words he chose to describe the level of their amazement. This was not just surprise or astonishment. The disciples were totally and utterly bowled over by what they saw Jesus do. The word 'astonishment' was usually used of the crowd in Mark, and described their emotions when they saw Jesus do something miraculous for the first time (see, for example, Mark 2.12). Mark's critique of the disciples here suggests that he thought that after having spent a long time in Jesus' company and especially after they had seen the feeding of the five thousand that they should not have been so astounded by his walking on the water.

The key can be found back in the previous boat experience when the disciples asked each other 'who then is this?' Two chapters later Mark thinks they should have been able to craft an answer to this question. If they could understand who Jesus was – who he really was – then his ability to walk on water should not have surprised them.

This brings us, then, to a second key characteristic of discipleship – the ability to have the proper expectations of Jesus based on a knowledge of who he was. I suspect we are no better at this than we are at not being timid. Our God remains far too small. We expect little of him and even when he does act we often omit to notice that he has. The challenge of discipleship is the challenge of recognizing at a deep level who Jesus really was and is, and of adjusting our expectations of him, the world and ourselves accordingly.

32

Mark 8.13–21 And he left them, and getting into the boat again, he went across to the other side. Now the disciples had forgotten to bring any bread; and they had only one loaf with them in the boat. And he cautioned them, saying, 'Watch out – beware of the yeast of the Pharisees and the yeast of Herod.' They said to one another, 'It is because we have no bread.' And becoming aware of it, Jesus said to them, 'Why are you talking about having no bread? Do you still not perceive or understand? Are your hearts hardened? Do you have eyes, and fail to see? Do you have ears, and fail to hear? And do you not remember? When I broke the five loaves for the five thousand, how many baskets full of broken pieces did you collect?' They said to him, 'Twelve.' 'And the seven for the four thousand, how many baskets full of broken pieces did you collect?' And they said to him, 'Seven.' Then he said to them, 'Do you not yet understand?'

Of all the exchanges between Jesus and his disciples, by far and away my favourite is this one in Mark 8.13–21. As we've seen already, coming as it does after the feeding of the four thousand, it is strongly reminiscent of the last time the disciples were in a boat with Jesus (after the feeding of the five thousand). This time, nothing miraculous took place, but then no discernible learning occurred either.

The first feature that jumps out of this passage is the way that the disciples and Jesus talked past each other. Jesus talked about the 'yeast of the Pharisees and of Herod'. Yeast was often regarded negatively within Judaism, and was thought to symbolize evil and corruption (which is why it is so striking that Jesus compared the Kingdom of heaven to it in Matthew 13.33), particularly the ease with which it could spread. Jesus' warning here was probably designed to remind the disciples of how careful they needed to be not to allow the suspicion and mistrust of the Pharisees and Herodians to infiltrate the ways in which they viewed the world.

The disciples, who were still, it seems, obsessed with bread, heard something else entirely. Their response is odd, to say the least. There is nothing in the text to indicate that Jesus had criticized them at all for not having the capacity to feed thousands of people – neither when Jesus fed five thousand nor when he fed four thousand – and in any case when they couldn't feed them Jesus had amply provided more than enough. Why then would they assume that Jesus was having a go at them for not bringing bread on a boat trip (even though they did, in fact, have a loaf)?

The answer seems to be that they were locked into a negative way of viewing themselves and the world around them. Jesus warned them to beware of the yeast of the Pharisees, and it might seem that that warning arrived too late. The disciples were already suspicious and mistrustful, and so heard important advice for living in the Kingdom as a criticism of who they were. It is so easy, when we allow ourselves to be swayed by the critical and negative views of others, to hear almost everything not as helpful advice but as personal criticism.

The most striking feature of what Jesus says, however, is his question to the disciples when they misunderstood him. At that point he asked them whether they could perceive or understand; whether they had eyes to see and ears to hear; and whether they could remember. The word 'understand' is repeated again from the conversation in chapter 6 and now added to perceiving, looking, hearing and remembering. The third key characteristic of discipleship includes, then, the ability to see what is going on, to make sense of it, to recall what else has happened, and hence to understand at a deep level the significance of what we have seen and heard.

The disciples had all the jigsaw pieces in front of them but could not put them together in any way that made sense to them. Instead all they heard from Jesus was criticism and rebuke. Of all the characteristics of discipleship this is the one that, for me, hits home the hardest. How often do we hear Jesus' gentle words of love as criticism? How often do we interpret his call to go out and spread the good news as a stick with which to beat ourselves? How often do we mistake sound advice for living in the Kingdom with reasons to feel bad about ourselves?

The greatest tragedy of all is that this mishearing of the message means that we, like the disciples, find ourselves failing to perceive, understand, see, hear and remember the glorious good news of Jesus. This is why perceiving who Jesus really is and understanding what this means for us and the world must stand as one of the most important of all characteristics of discipleship.

33

Mark 8.34 *He called the crowd with his disciples, and said to them, 'If any want to become my followers, let them deny themselves and take up their cross and follow me.'*

At this stage in the book, no one should really be in any doubt of the costliness of discipleship (if you ever were that is). The thread of costliness has been with us ever since our first exploration of the wilderness on the first day. Following Jesus requires us to be prepared to follow where he went – to go out into inhospitable wildernesses; to face testing and trials; to be challenged on our identity and calling; to leave behind the familiar and comfortable, and place following above everything else. Just in case any of us need a final sledgehammer of assurance, this is it. The choice to follow Jesus is a choice to take up our cross, just like he did.

The question is what this means in practice. This command is located in the context of the aftermath of Peter's declaration at Caesarea Philippi. In the run-up that we have been exploring in the boat narratives of chapters 4, 6 and 8, the growing problem was that the disciples simply didn't understand who Jesus was. In Mark 8.29, Peter finally declared what we have been awaiting for eight chapters – that Jesus was the Messiah. At last we can breathe a sigh of relief, at last one of the disciples – and Peter at that – has seen and heard, perceived and understood, and declared who Jesus really was.

But before we have even finished our sigh of relief, we discover that we have been a little premature. Peter understood that Jesus was the Messiah but refused to accept what this really meant. He accepted the title but not the identity of Jesus. Just like the devil, the Pharisees and those gathered around the cross, Peter wanted to define who Jesus was and how he should live out his vocation. He refused to accept that being Messiah meant that Jesus had to suffer and die (8.32). He almost certainly had a mental image of glorious military processions, might and splendour; not suffering, agony and death.

Jesus' response to Peter, and in fact to the whole crowd along with the rest of his disciples, was that not only was he, Jesus, called to accept suffering and death – but they were too. For Peter the news just got worse and worse. Not only did he have to give up his image of who Jesus was, he was called to accept that this would impact on his own life as well.

There are two parts to this call to deny yourself and take up your cross, though in reality the two are closely linked. The word 'deny' is used later in Mark's Gospel to refer specifically to Peter's dissociation from Jesus at his arrest and trial (Mark 14.30–31 and 72). In the Gospels it is only used of 'ourselves' (i.e. reflexively) here. Somewhat fascinatingly it is used in a similar way in 2 Timothy 2.13: 'if we are faithless, he remains faithful – for he cannot deny himself'. For God to deny himself seems to mean that he would be untrue to his nature. This sheds helpful light here. Denying *ourselves* requires us to dissociate from our nature: a nature that places ourselves and our concerns at the centre of our world; a nature that avoids suffering and death at all costs. Following Jesus requires us to go against the grain of human nature and to put someone else (Jesus) at the centre of our world. It requires us to be prepared to follow him, wherever he may go – even if that is in a crucifixion procession to death.

You will, of course, remember that none of Jesus' disciples followed him in this way. They fled long before they ever got to the crucifixion procession, though subsequent Christian tradition suggests that, decades later, many of Jesus' disciples did end up following Jesus in this way. The call to taking up your cross is not a masochistic, triumphalist call to 'death and glory'. Whether we take it in Matthew and Mark's versions (as here) or in Luke's ('let them deny themselves and take up their cross daily and follow me'), which suggests a more metaphorical image of self-sacrifice, the end result is the same. Jesus' call is not to death at all costs but a dissociation from the 'cult of me'. Two thousand years on the 'cult of me' reigns as supreme as it ever it did, and denying ourselves is no more straightforward than it was in Jesus' day. Despite 2,000 years of discipleship, it seems that we struggle to learn this most important lesson as much as the earliest disciples did.

34

Mark 8.34–37 *He called the crowd with his disciples, and said to them, 'If any want to become my followers, let them deny themselves and take up their cross and follow me. For those who want to save their life will lose it, and those who lose their life for my sake, and for the sake of the gospel, will save it. For what will it profit them to gain the whole world and forfeit their life? Indeed, what can they give in return for their life?*

The second half of Jesus' statement about discipleship has the feeling of a riddle about it: how do you lose your life while saving it at the same time? The simple answer is by following Jesus. That is where the simplicity ends. There is no doubt that it is best to treat this saying as a riddle so that the learning that we do comes about through reflecting deeply on it, wrestling with it, and through working out what it might mean for each one of us. A few insights, however, might kick start these reflections.

The first feature of this saying to notice is that in verse 34 Jesus used three imperatives: let them deny themselves, take up their cross and follow me. What can't be conveyed in English is that the first two of these (deny and take up) are in the aorist tense and the third is in the present tense. While it is important not to push this observation too far, by and large aorist imperatives refer to a single action and present imperatives to on-going action. In this case, then, we are called decisively and definitely to turn our backs on ourselves and to pick up our cross, and then to engage in the on-going activity of following Jesus wherever this may lead us.

Jesus goes on to say what this means using the words of this riddle. The clue to its meaning lies in verse 36. This phrasing of 'gaining the whole world' occurs in all three Gospels (Matthew 16.24; Mark 8.36; and Luke 9. 23); this is important because in Matthew and Luke 'gaining the whole world' is strongly reminiscent of one of the devil's tests – where Jesus was offered the glory of the whole world in exchange for worship. If you add into this the wider meaning of the Greek word translated 'life', then light begins to dawn. The Greek word used here is *psuche,* which can also be translated as 'soul'. Its wider usage in the Old and New Testaments suggests that it might best be translated as 'life-force' or 'who you really are'. Jesus was offered the whole world in exchange for who he really was – someone bound in deep and intimate relationship with the Father; what would he have gained if he lost that?

If we break into a paraphrase of – or riff on – this verse, then in my view it makes much more sense: 'If you want to be people who follow me, then deny your innate human nature: that which seeks self-preservation and self-promotion above all else. Those whose driving desire is to protect their life – with all its rights and privileges – will end up losing everything; but those who sit lightly to survival – so lightly, in fact, that sometimes they die – will, in doing so, discover who they really are. What is the point of gaining the whole world as a prize if, ultimately, you discover that you've lost yourself? When you've given yourself away, what is left to give anyone?'

It is the age-old lesson that Dr Faustus learnt in the oft-told legend when he sold his soul to the devil. Aiming for fame and glory – the whole world – can so grip and drive us that we lose ourselves in the quest. This is a lesson that reinvents itself in the life of every human being and needs learning again and again. The glamorous trophies and glittering prizes whisper to us, offering us the whole world in exchange for the simple gift of our souls. It is a powerful and dreadful seduction, easily accepted, but when we make it our goal, it turns to dust in our hands.

In today's language Jesus' call is to self-discovery. The

problem is that, like happiness, self-discovery cannot be achieved by direct approach. The quest for both happiness and self-discovery will, always, end in disappointment and failure. Like trying to hold a cloud in our hands, the more we try to capture them the more they will elude us. Discovering who you really are is only possible when you stop aiming for it. When you turn your back and walk away, embracing instead a life of compassion, love, and even suffering and death, then and only then can you discover your true identity. It is like the magical door in many a children's story; you can only find it when you stop looking.

Learning to lose your 'life' is counter-intuitive. It is a lesson that needs learning time and time again throughout our lives, and yet is profoundly and utterly true. Jesus invites us into an adventure of self-discovery, an adventure that we can only begin when we turn our backs on ourselves, and follow him in the opposite direction to suffering, death and beyond. This is the call of Jesus. It is a free and generous gift; it costs us everything.

This is the character and cost of discipleship. The two are intertwined – just as for Jesus in the wilderness there was no shortcut to being the Son of God. Miraculous provision of food, worshipping someone who was not God, and relying on God to save him from messes of his own making might have looked tempting temporarily but, as Jesus knew all too well, were the route away from the heart of his identity as the Son of God. In the same way, we are called as Jesus' disciples into the heart of the identity of being disciples, and on this journey, too, there are no shortcuts. We are summoned to life-denying sacrifice, and life-changing trans-formation. Jesus calls us to turn our backs on glory and success, and in laying down all our rights and privileges to discover that happiness and identity for which we yearn so much.

As we said all the way back in the introduction, a disciple is someone who learns to see the world through the eyes of his or her Rabbi. This requires of us the courage to lay down constant timidity and fearfulness, and to become people of deep understanding, who can see and hear the actions of God in our world, can remember all God has done, can perceive those actions for what they are, and understand what this means. It is this understanding that makes denying ourselves and following Jesus the only sensible course of action.

Questions for discussion and reflection

Reflecting on Scripture

- Read Mark 4.35–41; Mark 6.45–53; Mark 8.13–21.
- Leave a pause between each of the readings and then spend a minute or two in silence reflecting on what you heard.
- What themes jumped out for you from these readings? What did *you* hear Jesus saying to his disciples? Do you have a sense of what tone of voice he used when speaking to them here?

Discuss

The character of discipleship

- Think about the words/phrases from the three boat scenes that we explored.
  - Don't be timid/cowardly
  - They did not understand because their hearts were hardened
  - Do you still not perceive or understand? Are your hearts hardened? Do you have eyes, and fail to see? Do you have ears, and fail to hear? And do you not remember?
- If we use these as a guide for how we should live as disciples, what would this mean in practice? How would we live as individuals and as churches if we took this seriously?

The cost of discipleship

- What do *you* think it means to deny yourself and take up your cross?
- What is the difference, do you think, between Matthew and Mark's version ('taking up your cross') and

Luke's version of taking up your cross daily? Does one expect more of us than the other?

- Discuss Mark 8.34–37 what do you think Jesus was saying here? How can you lose your life in order to save it?

- Have a go at writing your own paraphrases of Mark 8.34–37 and share these as a group.

On wilderness and discipleship

As this is the last session of your group, spend some time thinking back over the past weeks.

- Is there anything that sticks out for you as particularly important for you?

- What do you want to take away and think more about?

- Are you going to do anything different in your daily life?

Epilogue

As we near the end of our Lenten journey to the wilderness and back again, we can see with clear insight quite what it is we have let ourselves in for. I don't imagine for a moment that Simon Peter, Andrew, James and John – or even Philip and Nathanael from John's Gospel – had the slightest inkling of what following Jesus was going to mean in and for their lives. If Jesus had spelled it out at the start there is a good chance that they might have decided not to follow after all. Unfortunately we are not in a position to discover what they thought about their decision to follow Jesus. All we can surmise from the fact that they never gave up and, after Jesus' resurrection and the sending of the Spirit, went to proclaim the good news of the Kingdom to the ends of the earth is that ultimately they decided that the cost was more than worth it.

Two thousand years later Jesus is still calling to us 'Come, follow me': follow me into the wilderness places and prepare for redemption and hope; follow me into a deep knowledge of your identity and calling so that you can stand firm in the face of trials and testing; follow me and I will teach you how to bring others to that moment of self-knowledge and decision; follow me in the way of the cross. It will require great courage and insight; it will require a counter-intuitive but decisive turning away from self-protection and self-interest; it will require of you far more than you think you have to offer; but as you journey deep into discipleship you will learn and change and be transformed, so that what before would have been unthinkable becomes natural in the footsteps of the one calling us.

When we talk about discipleship it can all too easily

become individualistic and inward-looking. If we truly follow in the footsteps of Jesus, then – like him – we will look beyond our own selves to a world in need of so much love and compassion. The journey of transformation that takes place as we learn from the Master calls us to see the world through the eyes of Jesus so that, to return to R. S. Thomas for a moment, as we look at it with its scorched land and crusted buildings, where people hold out their thin arms in hope, we find ourselves so moved with compassion that we cannot help the words tumbling from our lips … 'let me go there'.

Biblical Index